P9-DNZ-533

In Our Humble Opinion

In Our Humble Opinion

CAR TALK's Click and Clack Rant and Rave

•

Tom and Ray
Magliozzi

A Perigee Book

A Perigee Book
Published by The Berkley Publishing Group
A division of Penguin Putnam Inc.
375 Hudson Street
New York, New York 10014

First edition: May 2000

Published simultaneously in Canada.

The Penguin Putnam Inc. World Wide Web site address is
http://www.penguinputnam.com

Library of Congress Cataloging-in-Publication Data

Magliozzi, Tom.
    In our humble opinion : Car Talk's Click and Clack rant and rave / Tom
and Ray Magliozzi.
        p. cm.
    ISBN 0-399-52600-5
        1. American wit and humor. I. Magliozzi, Ray. II. Car talk (Radio program)
        III. Title.

PN6162.M246 2000
814'6—dc21   00-022351

Printed in the United States of America

10 9 8 7 6 5 4 3 2 1

To our wives, Monique and Joanne, without whose assistance, tolerance, support, tolerance, guidance, tolerance, inspiration, encouragement, and tolerance—did we mention tolerance?—this book of rants and raves would not have been possible . . .

•

To our children, Lydia, Louis, Alex, Andrew, and Anna, who mostly think we're nuts and without whom most of our ranting would not have been necessary in the first place . . .

•

And to Louie (Dad), and the memory of Lizzie (Mom), who provided us with a safe, happy place to grow up, instilled in us a strong sense of right and wrong, and helped us develop an ability to see things in a way that is quite different from the way most sane and rational people see them.

Contents

Introduction (Or Foreword? Or Reverse?)   xi

Preface   xiv

The Rant and Rave Primer   xvi

A Humble Beginning to Our Humble Opinions

Tom's Life Thus Far   3

Ray's Life Thus Far   11

Cars

It Won't Be Long Now . . .   23

I Can't Drive 55   29

Enough Is Enough!   36

Blatant Ergonomic Blunders   42

I Do Love Blue Hair, But . . .   48

Contents

There Aren't Nearly Enough Accidents:
Are You Doing Your Part?   52

Musings

The Parable of the Panhandler   59

Omean Aspiavodos   62

The Mystic Valley Boys   66

The Committee on Student Apathy   68

The IMM Syndrome   70

UFOs   74

Raising a Kid 101   78

A Seductive Plot of Enormous Complexity
and Brilliant Subtlety   83

The Theory of Abstract Cooking   89

A Taxonomy of Humankind   95

Progress Run Amok: A Parlor Game
for the New Millennium   102

Rants

The Penal Principle   111

A Bronx Tale—Sort Of   116

Help Us Overthrow the Tall/Short Mafia   121

The October Surprise: *"Just Say No!"* . . .
to 3:00 P.M. Sunsets   125

. . . And They Don't Even Break a Sweat!   128

Lies, Damn Lies, and Magazine Surveys:
A Surprising Result   131

And My **Brother** Has the Ph.D. in Marketing?   134

The Hollywood Manifesto   139

The Power of 2: Wherein the Automotive
Philosopher-King Discloses His Plan for World Peace   145

Contents

Percival Bananas: The Zoo Rant — 165

Monica What's-Her-Face and "Responsible" Journalism — 168

Another Microsoft Conspiracy — 170

The Deregulation of Airline Deregulation — 173

Walking — 177

Water, Water Everywhere — 179

Jock Itch? — 184

Going to the Dogs: Pit Bulls, Rottweilers,
and Testosterone Poisoning — 187

Half-Baked Science — 192

Stop the World—I Wanna Get Off!:
The Other Side of Road Rage — 198

The Andy Letter — 202

Bitch, Bitch, Bitch — 205

A Man Can't Just Sit Around — 209

The Wacky Way of Knowledge — 211

The Founding Fathers

The Founding Fathers: What a Bunch of Morons — 221

The Founding Fathers: Counter-Rant — 225

The Counter-Rant to the Counter-Rant — 229

The Education Trilogy: In Four Parts

Introduction — 235

The Trilogy — 237

Part I: The Allegory of the Epiphany at the Fountain — 239

Part II: A Scathing Indictment — 245

Part III: The New Theory of Learning — 255

Part IV: The Epilogue — 262

The Value of a Good Education:
(Dwayne and the Five Engineers) — 266

Introduction (Or Foreword? Or Reverse?)

You may have some misgivings about buying a book of someone's opinions—as well you should. After all, we all have opinions; and as we know, men have strong opinions about everything—especially topics they know nothing about.

Moreover, you have your own opinions, so why should you give a rat's patootie about ours?

Well, we can't offer any real guidance here, but we can at least tell you what some other people's reactions have been to our rantings and ravings.

Ray's Wife

In the midst of the writing of this book, Ray experienced a bout of writer's block. He expressed his concern to his wife, Monique, one day. "Gee," he said, "why would anyone want my opinion about anything?" To which she replied, "Look, Raymie, there's already a lot of real junk being published every day. You're just adding to the pile."

That seemed to do it for him, and he went back to writing.

Tom's Wife

Tom has been ranting for years. At first, Joanne would argue with his position—whatever it was. For example, she'd ask what evidence he had to support his position. Tom would say (in his best *Treasure of the Sierra Madre* accent), "Evidence? I don't need no stinkin' evidence." Tom has always felt that his logic is unassailable and evidence is therefore redundant, at best.

Now, when he starts to rant or rave, Joanne just rolls her eyes and says, "Oh, shut up."

Our Parents

When either of us goes into a rant with dear old Dad, he usually laughs. And then he tells a joke he first heard in 1918.

Whenever Tom unleashed a rant on his dear old sainted mother, her response was usually "What are you, crazy?" (This is the absolute truth.)

Given these reactions, all we can offer is the following:

Introduction

We wrote this book because someone actually offered to pay us to write it; i.e., they gave us an advance. We really don't expect to make any more money than they've already given us; so, if it makes you feel any better, none of the money you spend on the book will come to us. It will all go to the publisher—to help defray the expenses of the very big mistake they've made. Of course, you may or may not want to reward them for that mistake. It's up to you.

Last, we honestly don't mean to hurt anyone's feelings—unnecessarily; nor do we want anyone to be offended by what we've written—unless, of course, they deserve it. And in all cases, they do deserve it. In our humble opinion.

ha ha ha

Preface

(Tom Magliozzi)

I'm Tom—the older, smarter, more handsome brother (the one with a beard and a mustache). Ray is my baby brother. In all the years I've known him, I've never taught Ray anything; nor have I ever convinced him of anything. We're just two very different kinds of people. He's a hard worker while I'm a lazy bum. He loves sports. I hate not only sports, but also sports people and sports talk shows. Ray loves nature, and when he goes on vacation, he heads to the Grand Canyon or Muir Woods. As for me, give me a cup of espresso and a sidewalk café and I'm a happy guy. In my humble opinion, you've seen one tree, you've seen 'em all. There are virtually no areas of interest where Ray and I intersect.

Yet, there is one exception to all of this. There's one cosmic plane on which the two of us unite. The Rant and Rave.

Many years ago in a galaxy far, far away (actually, it was

during one of our radio shows), I broke into a tirade. I don't know what set me off; I think it had something to do with unscrupulous practices of one of the big three automakers. Actually, now that I think of it, I believe it was when Roger Smith, CEO of General Motors, retired. The Board of Directors gave Roger a retirement package worth millions of dollars. Now, here was a man who almost single-handedly had reduced the world's most powerful corporation to a shadow of its former self by virtue of his penny-pinching policies. If Roger could save 3 cents on a car part, he'd do it. The customer be damned. (This by the way, is the man who gave the world rear windows that wouldn't go down. His response? "If they don't like it, they can buy air-conditioning.")

You'd think the Board of Directors would throw this guy out on his ear and tell him not to let the doorknob hit him in the butt. Instead, they give him millions of dollars a year—forever! I went bonkers. I mean, I went on and on. I gave new meaning to the word "tirade." And so was born the Rant and Rave.

At first, my brother sat quietly while I vented, convinced that I had finally gone over the edge. But a few weeks later, it happened again. (I think it was Chrysler that time.) On this occasion, my brother sort of got into it. He urged me on to greater and greater heights. The next time, he actually contributed a little bit. By the fourth time he was right in there with me—side by side. And a few weeks later, it happened. Ray, my baby brother, the brother who loves trees more than concrete, sports more than espresso, broke into a spontaneous rant. Never have I been so proud. Finally we were brothers, in the true sense of the word. Click and Clack. Finally.

Ray still loves trees, but I'm working on that.

The Rant and Rave Primer

(Ray Magliozzi)

So, just what is it about ranting and raving that has the power to convert even me—the smarter, more handsome, saner brother? After much study, I've concluded that the power of the Rant and Rave lies in its cathartic action. Those gnawing events that plague our daily lives can fester and make us depressed if allowed to remain inside the human body. However, there is ample scientific evidence to suggest that through a process referred to in the psychological literature as "venting one's spleen," the body is cleansed and all becomes temporarily right with the world. This is the potent healing effect of the Rant and Rave. Body cleansing. Purging of the soul.

In this small book we offer therapy heretofore unavailable to the masses. We urge you to partake of it. You can start by simply reading. After perusing a few of our rants, you may find yourself nodding in agreement. Later you will begin to grunt approval. Then you will begin to explain the position taken in the rant to whomever is closest to you geographically, emotionally, or politically. In the next phase, you will find yourself rant-thinking; i.e., rants will begin to form in your consciousness. Unspoken, but fully coherent. Finally comes the eruption! Unplanned. Unexpected. A purely spontaneous explosion of your thoughts upon the world. The catharsis will cause an incredible lightness of being—to coin a phrase. You'll rant. You'll rave. Ahhhh!

Sometime later—maybe hours, maybe a week or a month—you will mutter to yourself (perhaps in the middle of dinner, or during a meeting with the Marketing Department), "Thank you, Tom and Ray."

You're welcome, my friends. You're very welcome.

If you listen to the show regularly, **AND YOU SHOULD**, you might feel you already know more than you care to know about us. If this is the case, might we suggest you skip right on ahead to the other sections, like our Rants. If this is not the case, and you'd like to know more then please read on and learn how this all came to be . . .

A HUMBLE BEGINNING TO OUR HUMBLE OPINIONS

Tom's Life Thus Far

I must admit, I'm a little reluctant to divulge all the following details about my life (especially considering all the fine work by the G-men who arranged to get me into the federal Witness Protection Program). But, here it is anyway.

I was born in East Cambridge, Massachusetts (yes, "Our Fair City"). I spent most of my "formative years," as they say, on Harding Street. This was the greatest neighborhood on the planet. Kids everywhere. Just hangin' out. Nothing much happened. Just good times. (My wife insists that if I had had a normal—i.e., abusive—childhood, I wouldn't be plagued with those continual bouts of raucous laughter.) I went to the Gannet School and then the Wellington School and then CHLS—Cambridge High and Latin School.

From then on, it was downhill; I went to MIT—or the "Toot" (or "Tute?"), as we used to call it. I turned down

Harvard, because MIT gave me 200 bucks more for scholarship money, and that was big bucks back in 1880.

Boy, I hated MIT. I worked my butt off for 4 long years. The only thing that saved my sanity was the 5:15 Club—named, I guess, for the guys who didn't live on campus and took the 5:15 train home. 5:15 my tush! I never got home before midnight! And when I say "guys" it's because back then, there were no females at MIT (to my knowledge, at least). I do remember some club that presumably was for female students. I never saw anyone easily identifiable as a female enter or leave the place. I walked around the campus in a complete funk for weeks, seeing only nerds; and I mean NERDS! Man, was I depressed.

Then one day I stumbled upon the 5:15 Club. Guys were laughing, yelling, shooting pool, and playing poker. I had found my home.

I actually managed to graduate and serve time in the U.S. Army. I could have been an officer. But I wasn't. I had spent several years in the Air Force ROTC and was recommended for the "advanced corps" (i.e., sign up for four years in the Air Force and we'll make you an officer). People told me this was quite an honor. I went to the interview. I flunked. And I know why. At one point, one of the very serious officers asked me this penetrating question. He says, "Cadet Magliozzi, when you entered MIT you had a choice of Army ROTC or Air Force ROTC. Why did you choose the Air Force?" I pondered for a moment and answered in all seriousness, "Because, Captain, I look so much better in blue than brown. Don't you think?" I got the rejection letter a week later. They couldn't take a joke.

So, after graduation, I had to do 6 months of active duty

to fulfill my Army Reserve requirement—or get drafted for 2 years! I spent my 6 months in Fort Dix, New Jersey, India Company, Fourth Training Regiment, with my good pals Sergeant McNeeley and Sergeant Torres. Boy, was I a great soldier. I was always in trouble because I couldn't shut up. I had KP (that's kitchen police, for you conscientious objectors) once a week. One night, from midnight to 6 A.M., I peeled 6,000 pounds of potatoes!

Every Saturday morning, after our little trek through the woods of New Jersey, Sergeant McNeeley would come into the barracks and announce, in his deep-fried Southern accent, "Everyone will go on pass this weekend . . . except Praaaaaavit Magggleeeeozzzzi." I'd laugh like hell. That really pissed him off.

After completing my 6 months of active duty (most of which I served as a cook) I entered the corporate world. I worked for Sylvania's Semiconductor Division in Woburn. Those were the days when everyone cheered when we got a transistor that worked. The important lesson I learned there was never take a job without first hanging around the place for a couple of days. What a lousy job.

Six months later I went to work for the Foxboro Company in Foxboro. This was good, mostly. I had a series of superb jobs, starting in the International Division, working for one of the sweetest people I've had the pleasure to know on this planet, a guy named Russ Milham. After a while, I became Far East administrator, visiting such wonderful places as Taiwan, Singapore, the Philippines. Then I became the company's long-range planner. What a great job. Feet on my desk, contemplating the future. (It was about this time that I discovered the secret of multiple offices. Whenever they couldn't find me, they'd say, "Oh, he must be in his other office." Right.)

You'd think that with a plum job like this I'd be in seventh heaven. But the schlepp was getting to me—an hour each way. I couldn't move to Foxboro, because it was Nowheresville. I HAD to live in Cambridge (My Fair City). BUT what finally did it was a tractor-trailer truck that almost did me in on Route 128 on my way to work one day. Shaking in my little MG-A after that experience, I asked myself a simple question, "If I had bought the farm out there on Route 128 today, wouldn't I be bent at all the LIFE that I had missed?" I drove to work, walked into my boss's office, and quit.

My boss was convinced that I had taken a job with a competitor. He just couldn't understand the actual truth. Life was the issue.

But I do miss the guys at Foxboro: Chick Nightingale, Doug Carey, Mike Huston, Norm Rice, Henry Desautel, Norm Robillard. Speaking of Norm Robillard . . . Norm decides one day that my life is not complete because I'm not a skier. So he's going to fix that. He takes me skiing one NIGHT after a FREEZING RAINSTORM and tells me, "It's easy. Don't bother with the lessons. Just follow me." I spent the night in the hospital and the next two months on crutches. I think of Norm often. Every time my knee collapses and I fall down in the street.

Anyway, two weeks after I quit the Foxboro Company, I was learning the fine art of "hanging out" in Harvard Square, drinking coffee. I did that for a year. Life was good. It's amazing how little money it takes to live when you don't have any (and don't want any!). Just the money I was saving not getting my shirts done was enough to live on. Odd jobs were the answer. Here is the best (1 of the 2 or 3 truly GREAT ideas I've had in my life). I was living in an apartment building that was loaded with single women. But how to meet them? Well, get this. If your apartment needed painting, the owners of the building would supply the paint, but they wouldn't supply the labor. I went into the painting business. My marketing effort consisted of a small sign in the laundry room: "I'll paint your apartment; $50 a room." (You may think $50 was too low. But it was all I could afford!) The phone rang off the hook. Life WAS good.

Another of the odd jobs I stumbled upon while self-unemployed was the International Marketing Institute. Would I mind going to Saudi Arabia for a month or two to teach in an executive development program? Would I mind? Were they kidding? I realize in retrospect that they couldn't find anyone who had a free month or two. Why? Because all the qualified people had what? Jobs! (I forgot to mention that while working at Foxboro, I had gotten an MBA and had been teaching part-time at various universities around Our Fair City.)

Anyway, I taught for IMI for many years, and got to see some of the more wonderful places on the planet. (Does the name Kuala Lumpur mean anything to you?) And to meet another one of the nicest guys I know—Jack Enright.

A LITTLE ASIDE: Every once in a while one of these exotic places would come up in conversations with Dougie Q. Berman (the esteemed producer of our radio show). I'd say, "I remember one time when I was in (insert some exotic place). . . ."

Dougie began to wonder under what circumstances I had visited all these places. So my brother and I concoct this story about my years in the CIA and how I'm now in the Witness Protection Program. Dougie buys it. Then Jay Leno calls and asks us to be on *The Tonight Show*. Dougie tells them that we can't do the show unless they agree to put one of those black dots over my face. After that, we told him the truth.

Anyway, life is good, I'm painting apartments and bopping around Kuala Lumpur, and then along comes my deadbeat brother. He had been teaching science someplace up in Vermont. And when the Vermonters ran him back over the border, he came to Cambridge looking for a job. I made the mistake of telling him about 1 of the 2 or 3 great ideas I've had in my life: a do-it-yourself auto repair shop. I had actually thought this up while at the Foxboro Company, contemplating long-term trends. I put together the trend of higher and higher auto repair costs with the fad of everyone (hippies, mostly) "getting into it," you know? And Budda-Bing-Budda-Bang, out comes DIY auto repair. "GREAT," says my brudder. "Let's do it."

"What are you nuts?" I say to him. "It's the W word. I don't go to W anymore. I drink coffee and paint the apartments of beautiful women. Flake off." But since he was totally unemployable and his wife was with child, he talked me into it. And so was born Hacker's Haven (that name was another of my truly great ideas). In those pre-PC (I mean personal computer, not politically correct) days, a hacker was someone who didn't know what the hell he was doing but gave it a try anyway. A haven for hackers. How sweet it is.

So we did it. We lost money, but we had a blast. And two very important events occurred during this time that make the DIY idea even better than great. The first was that since our business was new and different, people knew about us and we were asked to take part in a panel of automotive experts at WBUR, the Boston NPR affiliate. I was the only one who showed up (a panel of one?), and pretty soon the auto radio show was mine and Ray's.

Second, and even more important, I met the woman who is now my wife. WOW. What a woman! Suffice it to say that the web of coincidences, events, and luck that led to our meeting explains all we need to know about the cosmos, nirvana, and karma.

Also, to supplement my meager income at the garage, I worked a day or so a week at a small consulting company in Boston. Technology Consulting Group was a company owned by an MIT classmate of mine, Mike Brose.

So, there I was, garage mechanic, university instructor, and consultant. I was tired. It was beginning to feel like the W word. So, I sat down in Harvard Square one day and said, "How does one avoid the big W? Who makes a living without having to work?" And it came to me. College professors!

So, in addition to working at the garage, consulting, and teaching, I became a student in the doctoral program at Boston University. It took me 9 long years to earn the privilege of being called "Doctor."

By the way, while I was busting my cookies sitting at my computer day and night writing my dissertation, my wonderful daughter, Lydia, sends me a card with the following poem (for which you need to know that my initials are TLM. The T is for Thomas, the L is for Louis—after my father—and the M . . . well, you get the idea):

OH WHEN DEADLINES ARE CLOSE,
MOTIVATION IS LOW
AND YOU'RE WISHING FOR FAIT ACCOMPLI
WITH YOUR KEYBOARD IN HAND
AND YOUR NOSE TO THE SCREEN
PICTURE THIS . . . TLM, PHD

Finally I made it. I put on the robes, they called me "Doctor" (for one day) and I got a job as a real college professor. It was good. For about eight years. But suddenly (actually it happened gradually, but I didn't know it) it was over. I reached (through deep thought, meditation, and prayer) a miraculous epiphany. Teaching sucks. (This, too, is a long story; if anyone wants to know about my feelings regarding education, take at look at "The Education Trilogy.")

So I quit. The dean begged me not to, so I stayed. And THEN I quit again. And now I am fully quit. I'm very happy.

That just about takes me up to now. I'm doing the radio show, ranting and raving on the World Wide Web, writing half of this book, doing odd jobs (know anyone who needs her apartment painted?), and drinking coffee in Harvard Square. Some people ask if I've spent my whole life in Boston.

I say, "Not yet."

—**Tom Magliozzi**

Ray's Life Thus Far

Early to Bed, Early to Rise

I spent my early years in East Cambridge (Our Fair City). I was the quiet little brother. One of my earliest recollections was a brother, Tom, who was 12 years older than me. In fact, he still is. Tom, and my sister, Lucille, to this day say they didn't notice me until I was about 5 years old. Mom claims one morning Tom came into the kitchen and said, "Hey, who's this little kid who's always following me around?" I can't say that I remember much from my early childhood, except it was wonderful. I had everything a kid could want: two square meals a day, a basket to sleep in, and an imaginary dog. I do remember one thing, however: Mom always had us in bed at 7:00. If I was any kind of a person today, I'd be working this out in therapy. I never got to watch TV or do any of those fun things the other kids did. I'd lie in bed and listen to the sounds of my playmates outside. Talk about breaking a kid's heart. I was all tucked in with my blanky on a hot summer night, and they were frolicking in the streets. I think Tommy had to do the same thing, too. As a result of this, Tommy and I refuse to go to bed. When it's time to go to bed, you won't find us anywhere near a bed or under the covers. Sofas, chairs, kitchen table, you name it—anywhere but under the covers.

Grandma Pockets the Dough

I got my start in show business when I was 4 or 5. My grandmother (Mom's mom) lived with us, and Grandma's job was the shopping. Every day she and I would make the rounds to the bakery, the butcher shop, the grocery store, and at each stop it was up to me, little Raymie, to get out there and sing and dance for all the other grandmothers; all in Italian. I'd sing these songs from the old country, and all the old ladies would go nuts. They would throw all this money at me and my grandmother would pretend that I was getting it all. Then, when everyone left, she'd pocket most of it. She would keep 90% and give me 10%. She didn't understand the agent-talent relationship. All that change probably paid for that Lincoln Continental she bought.

I was a chunky little tyke. Mom says that Dad always wanted to call me Chunky but there was already a candy bar with that name, so they settled on Chucky, which I've been called, it seems, forever. I have cousins who, to this day, don't know my real name. No kidding.

A Humble Beginning to Our Humble Opinions

Taking Things Apart

For as long as I can remember, I've loved to take things apart to see how they work, and as a kid I'd take things apart and put them back together again, over and over. That was my hobby. Take it apart; put it back together again. The Museum of Science was right down the street from where we used to live, and Dad and I would go there almost every weekend. I got interested in being a scientist. Overall, I was pretty quiet as a kid, and my childhood consisted of standing around and watching Tommy take his car apart and then desperately try to put it back together again. Tommy owned a number of cars while we were growing up, all of which were complete junk boxes. As you might suspect, Tom has always owned cars that have been veritable heaps of automotive refuse. Some things never change.

Hide-and-Seek on the Mean Streets

When I wasn't hanging out with Tommy, I was playing all the regular kid games. We didn't have a park or playground to play in, and we certainly didn't have any grass. Our playground was the street. We played hide-and-seek and tag and stickball, and later on, spin the bottle. That was my favorite. Well, actually, playing doctor was my real favorite.

Our neighborhood was great because we had a million kids. I could literally walk out the door, and there would be kids everywhere to play with; it was great. The city was a lot of fun. You had the nice kids, the jerks, the weirdos, the tough kids, and I really got a lesson on how to deal with all kinds of kids. This may be the single most important thing that kids don't get if they grow up in the suburbs: everyone there is pretty much the same.

In the city you have to deal with everyone. There were some mean kids and there were some really nice ones, too. One of the first kids I met was from Italy. This occurred during one of my many years in kindergarten. This young fellow didn't speak any English, and he wore these funny clothes and little sandals—a lot like Tommy dresses today, come to think of it. I spoke a little Italian from all those songs I had to learn to buy Grandma that Lincoln. So we became fast friends until I moved away from Cambridge in fifth grade. One day, twenty years later, he came into the garage to fix his car, and of course I recognized him immediately. He was still wearing those stupid little sandals. It was nice to get reacquainted. We're now best of friends again; and, of course, his English is much better.

Heartbreak: A Case of Mistaken Identity

I went to the Gannet School for seven years. It was right around the corner from my house. It was a four-room schoolhouse, kindergarten through third grade. You do the math. One teacher for each grade. By the way, my siblings and our mother went to the same school, and I think we all had the same teachers. Anyway, my favorite teacher of all time was Alice Hughes. I had her for second grade and again for third grade, or maybe I was in second grade twice—I don't remember. Anyway, many years later at the garage, a customer named Mark

Hughes came in and said, "My mother would like to bring her car in." So, I say, "Sure, what's her name?" He says, "Alice. She's a retired schoolteacher. She used to teach right here in Cambridge a long time ago." And I thought this must be the Alice Hughes that I loved. So one day this little old lady comes into the garage, and I introduce myself. "Mrs. Hughes? Hi, I'm Ray Magliozzi. I think I had you as a teacher." She took one look at me and said, "No, I don't think so, sonny." Ah, it was a different Alice Hughes. I was positively heartbroken. I had been all prepared to cry in her arms and tell her about my pathetic little life. What a bummer.

The Third Brother: My Sister

My sister, Lucille, is a complete blank, as far as I'm concerned. I barely remember her. She was never home. I do recall, however, very vividly that she and Mom used to fight all the time when she was at home. You see, Sis was a slob. I remember many times when my mother would open up Lucille's bedroom window and throw all of her stuff onto the street. Her room was a mess, though, and I honestly can't say that she didn't deserve it.

Remember those pictures of houses in Florida that got hit by Hurricane Andrew? That's what Lucille's room used to look like all the time, stuff all over the place. Every once in a while, Mom would get sick of it and toss everything onto the street, Lucille would come home, see all her clothes and books strewn about the neighborhood, and then it was her turn to rant and rave. What a circus.

When I wasn't being amused by this, I would spend my time with Tommy, and even though I was just the little kid brother, he used to take me everywhere. He didn't always bring me back; he just took me places. He'd leave me there, and I'd have to find my way home. By the time I was 7, I had learned all the bus and subway routes in the entire city. Now I know this is my bio, but I'm going to include something that should have been in Tommy's bio that I'm sure he forgot to include. When my brother graduated from college, he joined the Army for 6 months. I think they call it the reserves. Then for the next 7 years he was supposed to go to summer camp. Well, one year he reported to Camp Drum in New York, and they didn't have his papers. They didn't know who he was or where he was supposed to be. So he got in his car and came home. They never called him back. Now that this tidbit of military intelligence is out, the Department of Defense is certainly going to come looking for him. Magliozzi, you owe us 7 years of summer camp. I can't wait.

Anyway, because my brother went to MIT, I guess it was predetermined that I would go there, too. I had no choice. And while I was there, I studied everything and really learned nothing. I eventually graduated from MIT in 1972. I ended up with a degree in humanities and science. MIT is known for its humanities program. After all, with a name like Massachusetts Institute of Technology, you know they must have a splendid humanities department.

A Humble Beginning to Our Humble Opinions

Sophomore Year Abroad

I took a year off in the middle of my MIT education and joined VISTA, Volunteers in Service to America. It was my sophomore year abroad, except I didn't go abroad; I went to Texas. And we did things like organize high school equivalency programs for adults, and we did some community organizing. It was pretty enlightening, all in all: basically we were radicals causing trouble.

Most important, it was where I met my future wife, Monique. Actually, we met in Norman, Oklahoma. We were doing all these little VISTA training games together. We met rappelling off a mountainside. I kid you not. I (cleverly) asked her to marry me while I was holding her safety line. She accepted, of course. We came back to Cambridge, got married, and Monique worked my way through a couple of senior years at MIT.

A Magliozzi in the North Woods

After college, I decided I wanted to try teaching. Why? Well, I knew I could do a better job than most of my teachers had done. So I got a job teaching science to unsuspecting kids in Bennington, Vermont.

Monique and I froze our butts off. We couldn't wait to get out of there. Between the snow, the mud season, and the blackflies, it was too much for us to handle. I will admit that I really did enjoy the fall. Fall in Vermont is awesome, both weeks of it. But man, winter sure comes on quickly and with a fury, and it stays a long time. My Mediterranean heritage just wouldn't allow it. What made matters worse was that Vermonters, at least the ones that we met, really weren't very friendly. I think you have to have a few generations buried there before they'll really accept you. It's probably different now, but we were definitely considered interlopers back then. Not only did we come from "someplace else," but we had a funny-sounding last name and I had this Cuban-looking dark skin. They probably thought I was smuggling cigars in from Havana. I was, but how could they have *known?*

How I Saved Thomas from a Life of Indolence and Vagrancy

So, there we were, Monique and I, in Bennington, Vermont, freezing all of our respective appendages off. At about the same time, Tom became self-unemployed. He was basically a bum, and he spent his days hanging out in Harvard Square, drinking coffee. I knew the best way to keep him out of trouble was to get him working, and Mom called me every day, begging me to rescue him. We decided to open Hackers Haven to save Tommy from a life of vagrancy. This was during the time when everyone was working on his own car, or so we thought, and our idea was to open a garage where people could do their own work and we'd rent space and tools to them. We knew our idea was brilliant and we'd have wheelbarrows full of money to show for it. Of course, the do-it-yourselfers who came in were such klutzes that we felt sorry for them, and we'd end up working on their cars for $2.50 an hour, which is what they were paying to supposedly do their own work. So we ended up fixing all the cars that came in. I mean, if some poor chump is spending all day trying to change his spark plugs, you can't help but give him a hand. Consequently, we ended up helping everyone all the time, and we made no money at all. We started hiring people to help out, and eventually the place just sort of evolved into what is now the Good News Garage. It was fun, though. We had some incredible laughs and we met some great people. We also met some weirdos, dingbats, and screwballs. This was Cambridge in the early '70s, and there were some real whacked-out people around then (and there still are).

I'll never forget this one guy, Joe Schram. We had this huge coffeepot that held 75 cups, and I swear he must have had 40 cups of coffee from that thing each time he was there. As you might imagine, by the end of the day, he was flying. I mean really flying. The longer he stayed, the faster he worked. Then one day Joe told us that he had to finish his car that day because he had to leave the state. Why? Well, he was being pursued by space aliens. Sure enough, he worked on that car all day, holding a coffee cup with one hand, turning the wrenches with the other; amazingly, the thing started up. We watched as he drove his car out the door, stepped on the brake pedal, and crashed that wreck into the building across the street. I'm sure those aliens caught up with him, because we never saw him again.

Monique, Andrew, Louis, Philly, and a Cat Named Doug

Monique and I have two kids. Andrew's 17 and Louis is 26. Louis has graduated from college and is gainfully employed; Andrew is at home screwing up the computer so I can't play Chessmaster. We get most of our companionship nowadays from Philly, our half–Border collie, half-everything else dog, and we love her. She was a stray we found while watching one of Andrew's Little League games. He played with the Phillies, hence the name. And, of course, we have Dougie the cat, named by Andrew after our esteemed producer, Douglas Q. Berman. These days I pretty much run the garage and work on *Car Talk*. The garage is still very much a full-time job. I get there at 8:00 in the morning or so and don't leave until . . . oh, maybe 9:00 in the morning. (Just kidding. I'm there all day.) I have four guys working at the garage, if you count both humans and subhumans. I'm still very much involved, and I still enjoy taking things apart and putting them back together again. Except now I can do it and actually charge for it. And I've gotten better at it over the years. Every time I do a job, I have fewer and fewer parts left over. What a great feeling! And of course, there's *Car Talk,* too. That consists of doing the show, driving all the new cars that come out, and trying frantically to come up with a mediocre new puzzler each week. I spend most of my time avoiding memos from our esteemed producer Doug Berman. He's always trying to professionalize us. If you've heard the show recently, you know he hasn't had a whole lot of luck—and I'm doing my best to avoid his advice.

—Ray Magliozzi

CARS

No matter what it is,

it's going to

cost you $200

if that's what it is.

It Won't Be Long Now...

Actually, it may be too late already.

Here's my opinion, as I sit pondering the cosmos whirling about me. What I see is disturbing; or maybe it's simply the natural order of things. What I see is a continuing deterioration of respect. Respect for people, authority, laws, rules—and ultimately, in my humble opinion—for civilized society.

After all, what is a society except a group of creatures (not necessarily human creatures) that has decided on a set of rules by which they will abide?

It's rather fragile. Who will decide which behaviors are acceptable and which are not? In the wild, it's usually the biggest and most powerful of the creatures who "decide." In human societies, the same is mostly true: The biggest and most powerful decide. We would hope, though, that in human societies, size and power will be somewhat tempered by reason—a characteristic that, we like to think, separates us from wasps, wolves, and the like. But maybe not.

In nearly all societies (including animal societies, primitive societies, and more sophisticated "advanced" societies), it becomes the responsibility of the "leaders" to teach others the difference between what is acceptable behavior and what is not. The mother lion teaches the cubs to be quiet when she—the mother—is on the hunt for food; in primitive societies, those exhibiting unacceptable behavior are punished or ostracized.

But what happens when a larger, stronger creature decides to challenge the norms of acceptability? Can it not replace the previously held views of acceptability with its own? In societies where groupings or coalitions form, cannot the new faction, given enough power, supplant the old views with new? And thus the society becomes different. Existing members of the society must either leave the group or learn to conform to the new rules.

In so-called democracies, the rules of acceptability appear to be determined not by the wisest members of the society but by the largest coalitions—be they wise, foolish, or something else. For it is their numbers, not their wisdom, that imbue them with the powers of leadership.

A Prediction—with a Warning— or Perhaps a Call to Action

In our society today the coalition with the largest numbers—or so it appears—is a coalition that is choosing to abolish the rules of respect. The members of this coalition are attempting to supplant existing rules of respect. Supplanting such widely held and accepted views in a society is a risky business. One may secretly hold a view that is deemed unacceptable—but how can one tell if one's views are shared by others? For, if he is alone, he risks being ostracized by the current leaders. To minimize this risk, he must "test the waters." One method of testing is to express the questionable view anonymously. If it elicits support, he can then identify himself as the source. If others object in large numbers, he is safe, since they know not whose view it is.

And where, in our current society, is one to find a veil of anonymity behind which to expose one's views? One relatively anonymous venue is the car. We see on our roads a spectacular display of selfishness and lack of respect and consideration for others—all anonymous. This disrespectful behavior is gaining the support of others who also care only for themselves. They support the position of disrespectfulness by following the lead of the new order—the Disrespecters. Every day their numbers grow. Their position is one of utter and complete selfishness, and appears to be this: Do whatever you want to do if it gets you what you want. Take whatever you want. Have no regard for the rights, feelings, or desires of others. If you must "push and shove" to get your way, so be it. If you don't feel like waiting for the light to turn green, don't. If you don't want to stop for the stop sign, don't. If you want to drive faster—much faster—than the law allows, go ahead. You will get away with it most of the time. And don't forget, you're anonymous. The police mostly won't see you, and those private citizens who do see you are powerless. Sure, they can report your behavior to the police, but the response from the police is "We can't punish someone for behavior we did not witness."

The risks of this behavior are few. Two things have changed in the past few decades. One is that most people used to behave in accordance with the rules simply because it was "the right thing to do." Conscience? Superego? These concepts are unknown to the Disrespecter.

Second, it used to be that the scofflaw was admonished for unacceptable behavior. The police gave tickets and respectable members of society ostracized the violators. No more. The violators now appear to be the establishment, and those attempting to follow the traditional rules are the ones being ostracized. Try to drive at the speed limit—you can't. On the highway that circles Boston (Route 95, formerly Route 128), the speed limit is 55 miles per hour. Hardly 1 vehicle in 100 follows this rule. Try it at your peril. Disrespecters will surround you, flashing lights, blowing horns, and making obscene gestures. The police do nothing. And it will get worse. Because as the Disrespecters gain numbers, and therefore power, they will expand their behavior beyond the roads. Leading ultimately to "If you want something   anything—take it."

It won't be long now. Actually, it may be too late already.

It seems that if any members of the old order—the Respecters—still exist, they are silent. Or frightened into paralysis. Unaware if they are still a majority or are now a small minority in the new order.

Should there be any Respecters still among us, it may be time to act. To take back the society we once had. We evidently cannot rely on the police to defend the old ways. They, too, have succumbed. They are not on our side. If something is to be done, we few must do it. Perhaps we will discover that our numbers are not so few. For we, too, have been anonymous. We have been frightened into the belief that we cannot identify ourselves as members of the old order for fear of reprisal from the new order.

But what to do? I've thought about this a little. Specifically about the behavior on the roads. In nearly all cases, we are indeed powerless. When a Disrespecter goes through a stop sign—cutting us off—he is soon gone. Should we chase him? And if we catch him, do what? If he cuts into a line of traffic illegally, he is, again, ahead of us and soon gone. Anonymously gone.

It occurs to me that there is only one situation where we have a slight advantage: being tailgated. It is the only situation in which we have the position of power, for we are in front of the perpetrator. The only time when we might possibly be able to exercise some semblance of control. It seems to be the only situation in which we can identify ourselves as members of the old order and, in so doing, seek support from other members of the old order. By identifying ourselves, we offer an opportunity for others also to identify themselves.

And to make a statement: "We are members of the old order. The old order is powerful. The old order will not allow or condone the behavior of the Disrespecters. We are many. We have greater numbers than you."

What can we do?

There are various approaches. Here are some:

We could, for example, express our disapproval to a tailgater by immediately slowing to a crawl. We could use bumper stickers to identify ourselves as the old order. And since there is strength in numbers, we would gain new power by identifying ourselves. On roads like Boston's Route 128, we could form a "moving roadblock" traveling at the speed limit. Doing the job the police refuse to do. Will it cause chaos? Sure. But what do we have now? What will we have soon? Don't forget that soon Disrespecters will no longer be concerned with anonymity and their despicable behavior will not be limited to their cars. Soon they will be breaking down your door.

Stop them—now while there is still a chance.

It won't be long now.

Maybe it's already too late.

I Can't Drive 55

(Ray)

When I was a little kid, like eight or nine years old, I remember reading a story in *Popular Science* magazine, or maybe *Popular Mechanics*. Basically the story was about new cars. Oh, these weren't the '56s or the '57s. These were real cars of the future. These cars were going to be like cars we had never seen before. They were going to hover above magnetic tracks embedded in the road, and they would be conveyed along superhighways, with computerized guidance systems. You would tell the car where you wanted to go and it would simply take you there without your driving it. These cars of the future even had things like collision avoidance systems and other high-tech stuff, and they would also be equipped with reclining seats and TVs. The occupants would be whisked along safely in comfort equal to that of their own living rooms, and would arrive at their destinations relaxed and refreshed in complete computer-controlled safety. Wow! When you neared your destination and you had to get off this magnetic superhighway and use the secondary roads, conventional wheels would descend from the car's body. Then you could continue your drive to Grandma's house by electric motor propulsion, your batteries having been charged up by magnetic inductance during the highway portion of the trip.

I remember thinking how awesome this was. Man, it was cool, and it all seemed so doable. Oh, I almost forgot to mention the best part. The author claimed that the vehicles would travel close to the speed of sound, and all this would happen in, like, the next 50 years.

OK, well, I lied about that speed of sound stuff. That wasn't true, but the rest is true, I swear it. I remember reading the article like it was yesterday. And I was so excited about this prediction, I went to sleep every night for a week dreaming about it. Maybe this was the thing that got me interested in cars. I think I peed the bed three nights in a row, too. I mean, this was really exciting stuff. Well, here it is almost 45 years later, and boy, was that guy wrong! We'll probably put men on the moon long before those future cars are ever seen. (You don't believe that we actually put a man on the moon, do you? That was a giant hoax perpetrated by NASA and the media—in my opinion.)

Maybe I'm just bummed out that here it is the year 2000 and it takes longer than ever to get to Grandma's house and those cars that were promised are nowhere to be found. I was a little kid. It was cruel. That writer shouldn't have done that to me. I was looking forward to those cars, and I still am. Those cars were promised to us. It was going to happen in 50 years, the guy said. What a jerk.

Now I don't want anyone to get the wrong idea or anything. Just because I'm disappointed about the nonavailability of these high-speed, futuristic automobiles doesn't mean that I drive like a nut. I am disappointed that we're still driving 55 and we still have to actually turn the steering wheel and look at the road, but I will confess that when I'm on the highway, I often drive at speeds over the posted limit.

Now before you get your tights in a bunch, I'll tell you why, and more important, I'll tell you why I'm very concerned about the 55 mph speed limit. Not long after reading that article, I remember taking a trip with my parents to Tanglewood, which is out in western Massachusetts. And to get there, we drove on the Mass. Turnpike, and the speed limit on the Mass. Pike—are you ready for this?—was 70 miles an hour. And we made that trip at 70 miles an hour in a '59 Rambler or some other car from the Jurassic period. This was a car that had no antilock brakes, no air bags, no radial tires. It didn't have four-wheel independent suspension. In fact, I'm not sure it had a suspension system at all. It had no seat belts, no energy-absorbing bumpers, no disc brakes, no rack-and-pinion steering, and no padded dashboard. In fact, if you can remember the old cars, they all had steel dashboards. When you hit your head against that dashboard, you were a goner. And yet the 70 mph speed limit was considered OK.

Now I will admit that there were fewer cars on the road then, but those old cars, by today's standards, were death traps. And yet the authorities allowed us to drive at 70 miles an hour. Of course, that was the speed limit. There were plenty of people driving 75 or 80, just like today. Then along came 1973 and the Arab oil embargo, and because supplies of gasoline were short, our leaders, i.e., Congress and the President, had to come up with an idea to conserve gasoline. And they came up with the 55 mph speed limit. I guess they felt that the 55 mph speed limit was a good compromise because it would conserve gas. Perhaps not as well as the 35 mph speed limit that my brother has espoused for all these years, but it did save gasoline while still allowing people to get to work on the same day that they left their homes. It was a good idea, and most people really did their part and drove 55. I know I did—especially when my wife was in the car with me.

Shortly thereafter the Arab oil embargo ended, but the 55 mph speed limit stayed. Yet there are many roads that I drive on today where I can't go more than 55 because that's the speed limit, except people are whizzing by me at 75 and 80 mph with impunity. Our nephew, who drives from New York to Boston all the time to visit his mother, our sister, tells us that he drives at 75 and everyone is passing him like crazy while he's making his trip. He sees no fewer than three or four state police who are either driving along with the flow of traffic or sitting by the side of the road, letting everyone go by. This is dangerous, but not for the reason you think.

When our government imposed a 55 mph speed limit, it was designed to save gas, but they soon realized that it saved lives, too, and that was great. But I know the 55 mph speed limit is no longer responsible for saving lives. How could it be? Everyone's driving 75 or 80. In fact, only a handful of people are driving 55, and my brother is one of them. Now my brother is a wonderful guy, but he doesn't obey any rules of any kind except speed limits. So he gets on the highway and he's bound and determined to make everyone drive at 55 because that's what the speed limit says. So he gets out in that left-hand lane, and he drives at 55 mph, maybe even 54. Of course, no one can pass him. Why? Because they'd be speeding. And he wants to make sure that he teaches everyone a lesson as he drives at 55 while almost everyone else wants to drive at a speed greater than this. So he is a moving road hazard. He's creating a problem, and other people like him that are for whatever reason determined to uphold the law, determined to do what they can to make sure that everyone else does not drive over the speed limit, are creating a dangerous situation on our highways. As well intentioned as they are, and as committed to setting a good example for their kids about obeying the law, they may be more responsible for road rage and accidents than they could ever imagine. They're trying to do the highway patrolman's job, and in doing so, are infuriating everyone else.

Yes, I know they're right, but these Rambler-driving vigilantes are not the police. If the police aren't going to enforce the 55 mph speed limit, then why are guys like my brother trying to do it? It's not their job. But as much of a pain in the butt as they are, they're not the real danger. The real danger in allowing people to drive at 75 when the speed limit says 55 is that it creates disregard and contempt for the law. People who are driving 75 and pass a state police car or a highway patrolman who doesn't pull them over begin to feel that the rules don't mean anything, and if I don't have to obey this rule, maybe I really don't have to obey any of the other rules. Maybe the police are just out there for show.

So by allowing people to speed, we have created a situation where we are encouraging people to have disregard for the law, and that's what's dangerous. If you're going to make a law, enforce it, and if you decide for whatever reason not to enforce it, then change it. And 75 mph is an OK speed limit in my humble opinion. Furthermore, I think in places where the cattle population outnumbers the human population, or even if it's close, the speed limit ought to be 85.

You know, it really bothers me that each and every time I break the speed limit, I'm setting a bad example for my kids. We're all doing it. We're in effect telling our kids it's OK to break the law, and you can pick and choose the laws you want to obey. Do whatever works for you. This, perhaps, is why no one takes the laws seriously in our country. Is it any surprise, then, that we have people talking on cell phones, reading the newspaper, putting on makeup, or eating breakfast while driving? We already have anarchy on our roads. Nobody obeys the rules, but let's change that. Let's start by changing the speed limit and then enforcing that speed limit. Let's make it so the police will enforce it and the other rules of the road. Let's encourage the police to ticket more tailgaters and arrest more drunks, and let's get my brother out of that left-hand lane and into the breakdown lane, where he belongs.

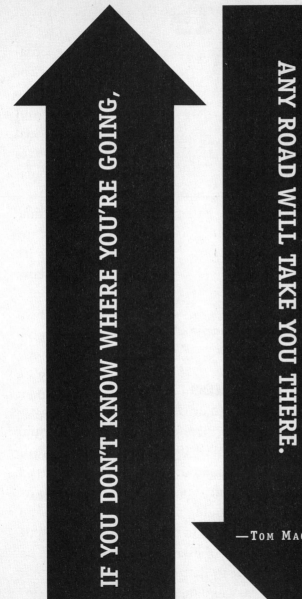

IF YOU DON'T KNOW WHERE YOU'RE GOING,

ANY ROAD WILL TAKE YOU THERE.

—TOM MAGLIOZZI

Enough Is Enough!

(Tom)

An Open Letter to the "People in Charge" at All the Auto Companies

Listen up, because I ain't kidding.

Recently I had occasion to drive a BMW M Roadster (the souped-up version of the Z-3), and although I used to think I'd never meet a convertible I didn't like, I didn't like it; mostly because it is grossly and unnecessarily overpowered. That got me thinking about other unnecessarily overpowered vehicles that really shouldn't be on the road. After all, they serve no purpose other than to get people into trouble, into accidents, and into the obituaries. (Keep your pants on. I know about fun. I'll get to that part.)

Just why are these cars so dangerous and why is the production of them so irresponsible? First of all, the fatality

statistics show them to be dangerous; fatal accidents with
Outrageously Powered Cars (OPCs for short) are about
twice—in some cases three times—those of more reasonably powered cars (you can see for yourself on the Highway
Loss Data Institute Web site at www.carsafety.org). Why is
that? Speed? Not entirely. The truth is that you don't need
outrageous horsepower to obtain outrageous speeds. Most
reasonably powered cars will go well over 100 miles per
hour—plenty of speed for getting yourself killed. The real
problem is acceleration—i.e., how long it takes to get to the
speed that's going to kill you.

"Normal" cars will go from a dead stop to 60 mph in
about 10–12 seconds; i.e., you floor it and hope nothing is
in your way. Zoooom. Ten seconds later you're doing 60.
And the acceleration (rate at which your speed is increasing)
is such that you can't control the car. (I do not suggest that
you try this. If nothing else, it's very scary.)

In an OPC, you can reach 60 mph in 3 to 4 seconds!
Think about it. You're at a dead stop and 3 seconds later
you're doing 60. And in the OPC you truly cannot control
the car. In fact, at the rates of acceleration that one can attain
with an OPC, it's difficult to control the car at almost any
speed. And that's what gets you into trouble. (Proponents of
the OPCs claim that the increased acceleration allows them
to get out of harm's way in difficult situations. The truth is
that they would never have gotten themselves INTO the difficult situation in the first place if they hadn't been driving
such a ridiculous car.)

Here's the other problem. The Outrageously Powered
Car MAKES you drive fast. Even if that's not the way you
usually drive. I have always contended that even Mother

Teresa would have driven like a nut if you put her in a Corvette. I am a conservative driver, and even I—known to my friends as 35 mph Tommy—drive like a nut when I'm behind the wheel of such a car.

As Americans, we've been taught to believe in the power (and the sanctity) of the "free market." Except in rare cases, we don't want the government sticking its inept, corrupt nose into our business. We won't accept governmental controls that would prohibit Ford from manufacturing a Mustang Cobra—or Chrysler a Viper, or GM a Corvette. Our belief is that the free market will take care of things. If people don't want it, Ford (or Chrysler or GM or Toyota or BMW) won't make it.

Personally, I don't completely agree with this philosophy. It allows individuals and companies to pander to the lowest levels of intelligence and the highest levels of bad taste. In the media, it gives us the likes of Jerry Springer. Jerry Springer and Vipers don't make us a better people, nor do they make this country a better place to live. But Jerry Springer is only Jerry Springer, whereas in the case of automobiles we have an entire industry from which we have the right to expect more. We expect highly paid, presumably intelligent executives to have the intelligence and wisdom to go beyond the anything-for-a-buck mentality.

Some of us had the audacity to think that the horsepower wars of the '60s were mercifully coming to an end. On the contrary, the trend is definitely in the opposite direction. BMW, which had a perfectly fine sports car in its four-cylinder Z-3, felt the need to turn it into an Outrageously Powered Car. Mercedes is getting power-crazed. Even mild-mannered Toyota is touting the power of its vehicles. And the VW Bug! With a turbo? The Viper—along with the people who produce it—makes me puke.

Am I just an old fart trying to take away people's freedom and their joie de vivre—the enjoyment of driving a sporty car? I don't think so. I have owned an MG-A, a TR-6, an MG-TD and a Fiat Spider. (And you certainly have to be a "sport" to drive a Fiat!) One doesn't need excessive, unnecessary horsepower to have fun driving. A sports car doesn't need to have 350 hp to be a sports car. Is the Miata not far more of a sports car than the current Mustang? And let's not forget that the car that introduced a sports car "for the people" was the 1964 Mustang. Hundreds of thousands were sold with a perfectly adequate 6-cylinder engine (145 hp, I think).

So, what can we do to fight the sanctity of the free market? First, we have to accept that no matter how highly paid and intelligent the automotive executives may be, it appears they can never be trusted not to succumb to the siren call of the almighty buck. Given that fact, they simply can't be trusted to "do the right thing." It's hopeless. If they exhibit no moral sense, then I suppose those who do have some sense have the right to tell them, and to attempt to stop them.

If we are constrained by the "sanctity" of the free market, the automobile industry will continue to make ridiculous, dangerous vehicles as long as someone buys them. And as we well know, there will always be testosterone-poisoned buyers.

So here's the plan devised by my clever brother and me: You want to make them? OK, go ahead. And the morons want to buy them? Go ahead. But we, the people, don't have to allow you to drive them on the roads that we use.

That is, we won't allow you to register them!

Here's my plea.

I'm looking for a few brave, levelheaded politicians—whom the auto and oil companies don't have in their pockets—to help me write legislation that will prohibit the "registration" of certain vehicles. It turns out to be easy to identify such vehicles. You can't just limit horsepower, because big, heavy vehicles do need lots of horsepower. What we need to do is prohibit vehicles that exceed a maximum horsepower-to-weight ratio. Here are some numbers I found on www.cars.com that got the information from the manufacturers (all based on '99 models):

VEHICLE	HP/WEIGHT RATIO
BMW M Roadster	.08
Mustang	.07
Mustang Cobra	.09
Corvette	.11
Camry	.04–.06
Toyota Supra	.09
Chevy Suburban	.05
Taurus	.05
Miata	.06
Volvo V70	.06
Dodge Viper	.13

It's pretty easy to identify cars that shouldn't be on the road. A horsepower/weight ratio for sensible cars—cars that have plenty of power, by the way—is 0.06, in my humble opinion. Note that the Suburban (with a 255 hp engine) has a ratio of only .05 because it weighs more than 5,000 pounds. The ridiculous Viper, weighing 3,400 pounds, has 450 horsepower.

I'm now working with my state representative to initiate legislation that will prohibit the registration in Massachusetts of vehicles which exceed the .06 HP/WT ratio. If you want to do the same in your state, give your state representative a call.

You can find your state legislators on the Web at: http://www.piperinfo.com/state/states.html.

Thanks for listening.

Blatant Ergonomic Blunders

(Tom)

Until recently, I drove a magnificent 1963 Dodge Dart convertible. To my mind, it was the epitome of simplicity and functionality. For example: Heater controls were three big round knobs. It was easy to remember which knob did what, and I could always tell which knob I was touching even in the dark.

Nearly 40 years of technological progress have brought us to an era in which it appears that nearly all automotive designers seem to have forgotten the lessons that they should have learned at the knees of their (far more intelligent) predecessors. One would think, for example, that Ergonomics 101 would make it quite clear that people using the controls in a car are otherwise busy: they're driving a car, for God's sake! The controls should not demand all their attention;

i.e., you don't make controls that REQUIRE the driver to take his eyes off the road. Duh.

I recently drove a car that for some reason needed 14 buttons to accomplish what was done by the 3 knobs in my Dart. (I won't mention any names; we have enough lawsuits pending. OK, it was a GM car.) Not only did this Buick (oops) have 14 buttons, but they were all exactly the same size and shape, and all perfectly flat, so as to be totally indistinguishable by touch (meaning that one had to look at the miniature icons stenciled on each button to determine its function).

Unfortunately, mistakes like these seem to be the rule rather than the exception. We test-drive 50 to 100 new cars a year, and I am struck by the proliferation of blatant ergonomic screwups. I've been pondering the situation, and it seems that there's a pattern to these mistakes. So, I would humbly like to suggest a Taxonomy of Blatant Ergonomic Blunders. Here are the categories:

1. Use a technology not because it's appropriate, but because "it is there." (I call this the Sir Edmund Hillary School of Ergonomics.)
2. Be different at any cost.
3. Reinvent everything.
4. Copy nothing; not even great ideas. It's embarrassing to admit that you didn't think of it yourself.
5. Just plain stupidity. (I call this one the Ted Williams Theory. He once advised a not-too-bright teammate, "If you don't think too good, try not to think too much.")

6. Too many cooks.

7. Oops! Where the hell are we gonna put this?

Consider these examples. A few years ago, I climbed into a mid-size American-made sedan with power everything. The seat controls were in the traditional location on the bottom left side of the driver's seat. But, when I reached down to adjust the seat, my hand didn't fit between the seat and the door. I had to open the door to adjust the seat! Clearly a category 6 mistake—Too many cooks. The designers of the door never bothered to talk to the designers of the seat controls. No big deal, I thought; there will be complaints and bad reviews, and common sense will prevail. They'll fix it next year.

The following year, the seat controls had indeed been completely redesigned. First of all, they were no longer the classic 2 buttons (or 3, if you get the lumbar control. We all need to control our lumbars, don't we?). No, instead of 2 (or 3) buttons, the seats were now controlled by 9—count 'em, 9 buttons. Nine flat, identical buttons. (Category 3, Reinvent everything?) And where to put these 9 flat identical buttons? Well, there really was no place to put 9 buttons. Ah, but the car had a center console between the bucket seats, and they put their fancy new buttons on a vertical plate at the back end of the console—toward the rear of the car (category 7—Where the hell . . .). Were these controls awkward to reach? Just try touching a spot on the back of the chair that you're sitting on with your fingertips. Easy?

It gets better. Assuming you can reach the buttons without chiropractic intervention, which button to press? To see the hieroglyphics stamped on the buttons, it was necessary not only to take my eyes off the road, but also to look toward the back of the car! While I'm driving! What were they thinking?

This seat control debacle is especially sad considering that many years ago, Mercedes Benz designed the ultimate in power seat controls that will surely go into the Seat Control Hall of Fame for beauty, simplicity, and pure elegance. "If you want to control a seat," they must have said, "why not make a control that looks and feels like a seat?" Indeed.

Can you do any better than that? Should you even try? Did all other manufacturers immediately jump on this brilliant idea? Ford, to its credit, was the first to copy it. But Chrysler? Volvo? Even the Japanese—who built their reputations by copying stuff? No, no, and no. And GM? Buttons. Flat, indistinguishable buttons (a classic Category 4, Copy nothing).

(**NOTE:** As of this writing, most manufacturers have finally admitted their complete failure in seat controls—after a decade or so—and have managed to overcome their stubbornness. There are still a few holdouts, but I won't mention any names. It reminds me of Jerry Seinfeld's comment regarding the Chinese persistence in using chopsticks. "After all," he said, "they've seen the fork!")

The car radio is another area of technology run amok. One rule of thumb seems to be "the cheaper the radio, the better the controls." More money gets you technological overkill. Like a graphic equalizer. A graphic equalizer? Graphic? In a car? At the other extreme we have tiny, tiny buttons. I think Volvo has changed the design, but the last one that my wife owned had 6 teeny buttons performing various functions. The total surface area of the 6 buttons was a little less than the surface area of 1 finger. It was virtually impossible to touch only 1 button at a time unless you carried a toothpick with you. I suppose the Swedes figured it like this: "Every one of these teeny buttons does something wonderful. Why should you care which one gets pressed. Take a chance! Lighten up."

So, just how far can designers take their obsession with inappropriate technology? The answer came from—of course—GM. (And others have actually copied them. Lexus, for example.)

Here's what I think must have happened at that great Center for the Ergonomically Challenged (a.k.a. the General Motors Technical Center in Warren, Michigan):

"Why not," they must have mused, "put the controls for everything in one place?" How might one do that, you might ask. Their answer? "Why, on a touch-sensitive screen, of course!"

If you want to turn on the heater, you press the menu item that says Heater Controls. Then you get a new screen with Temperature, Fan, Air-conditioning, Vents, etc. Say you choose Temperature. You get a screen that says Up and Down. So, you go up a bit. But you don't know if that's what you want because the fan isn't blowing hard enough. So you go back to the original menu.

("Let's see, how do I get back to the original menu? Let's try this. No, that's not it. How about . . .") Insert here the sound of screeching brakes, a horrible crash, metal tearing at your flesh, flames engulfing . . . Well, you get the idea.

"Whoopee!" they all (must have) cried out. "Whoopee!"

This touch-screen technology takes the multibutton philosophy to a whole new level of stupidity. For one thing, it can display thousands of buttons! And these buttons have no discernible edges at all! You have no chance of finding the buttons without taking your eyes off the road. Can you feel a pixel? The touch-screen technology was used Because It Was There (Thank you, Sir Edmund Hillary)—not because it made any sense.

These are just a few of the blunders I've noticed. I keep asking myself "What are they thinking?" Is it that they just aren't thinking? Or if they are, they just aren't thinking too good—so they shouldn't be thinking too much. I don't know.

Maybe they'll get the idea when they find out that I have instructed my heirs to sue the sorry butt off the manufacturer of the car that I'll be driving when I go to that big used car lot in the sky. Because I know the accident will have happened while I was feeling around for a pixel—or equalizing my graphics.

I Do Love Blue Hair, But . . .

(Tom)

Here's an issue someone has to talk about—but nobody seems to want to. It's the question of Old Folks and Driving. This seems to be a very sensitive subject. Not a politician in the country even wants to think about it, never mind talk about it—and never mind *do* something about it. But someone has to do it, so here I am.

Old people—love them as we do—really have lots of accidents. The vehicular fatality rate among people 75 and older is almost as high as that of 17-year-olds. The accident rate is probably off the charts, but I can't even find a chart!

Here's the problem. We all want to drive . . . well, almost all of us. It gives us power and mobility, and therefore freedom and independence. But some of us just shouldn't be allowed to drive. In our hearts, we all know that. Driving is not a right; it's a privilege. A privilege that must be earned. That is, you have to prove that you're capable. After all, we don't allow 10-year-olds to drive. Why? Because they don't have the physical capabilities or the good sense to handle it.

As we age, we lose both our physical capabilities and our good sense. Yet, in nearly every state of the U.S., all one needs to do is pass a vision test every 5 years or so in order to continue driving legally. A couple of states are considering stricter requirements for the elderly. To my knowledge, none has actually done something about it.

Of course, you know why no one wants to address this issue: it's politics, of course. Old people vote, and in great numbers—so just about every elected official, the only ones who have the power to do something about this—won't touch this question with a 10-foot pole. The elderly have an extraordinarily powerful lobby. First, there's the American Association of Retired Persons. I don't know this for a fact, but I'd be willing to bet big money that the AARP lobbyists are quietly telling legislators to leave this alone if they want to get reelected. In addition, AARP members would drop their memberships in a New York minute if they knew that the AARP gave the slightest hint that they shouldn't drive. (AARP, however, does have a pamphlet containing guidelines for the elderly to test themselves to determine if they should continue to drive.)

And where is the American Automobile Association on this issue? Why aren't they supporting a movement for stricter licensing requirements? Just another example of the good old boys (yeah, and you, too, good old girls) shirking their responsibilities because it might cost votes.

When your reflexes go, you can't stop when that kid runs out into traffic. (Please, God, don't let it be *my* kid, we all say. But it's going to be someone's kid.) When your sensibilities go, you lose track of where you are and what you're doing. (Please, God, don't let the old guy stop in the middle of the freeway and cause a 20-car pileup in front of *me*. But it's got to be in front of someone.) It isn't rocket science. Everyone knows what's right, and everyone is hiding.

If you don't want them to hide, how about we all write to our elected officials who can—and should—be doing something about this? This is not a federal issue. Individual states determine the rules for driving. So we need to write to our state legislators.

Please write. We've made it easy for you. You can find the names of your state senators and representatives at http://www.govnetworks.com/legislat.htm. We wrote a simple letter that you might want to copy.

Dear _____:

I've been very concerned for a long time now about the fact that there are no special rules regarding the issuance of driver's licenses to the elderly. As we all know, age brings physical and psychological problems that make us less able to cope with the difficulties and uncertainties of driving. This puts us all in danger— especially pedestrians, and most especially young children and (ironically) elderly pedestrians.

We are joining others in an effort to get something done about this very serious issue. We realize it will take courage on your part, given the powerful lobbying efforts of the elderly. But please search your heart and do the right—rather than the political—thing.

Do you personally have any plans to look into this issue?

Thank you for listening.

Tom and Ray Magliozzi
Hosts of *Car Talk* on National Public Radio

There Aren't Nearly Enough Accidents: Are You Doing Your Part?

(Tom)

The reason there are so many traffic accidents is that there aren't nearly enough traffic accidents.

The paragraph above represents the kind of in-depth thinking that goes on here at Car Talk Plaza.

And what we have here is possibly a Zen koan, maybe just an interesting paradox, or perhaps simply the raving of a crazy old man. You be the judge.

But first, allow me to explain.

If you take the time (as I did) to look up the definition of "accident," you'll discover that it means an unforeseen—or unexpected—event. Thus, if an event is foreseen or expected, by definition it isn't an accident. But unforeseen by whom? If the "incident' is unforeseen by some snot-nosed teenager, can it be considered an actual accident? Or was it simply unforeseen by someone who unforesees just about everything and therefore doesn't count—and therefore IS foreseen and therefore is not an accident?

My contention is this: most of the automobile "incidents" that we typically refer to as "accidents" aren't really accidents at all, simply because you'd have to be a complete moron to NOT expect them. Allow me, if you will, to elucidate.

We have certain mechanisms in place to help prevent—or at least reduce the likelihood of—accidents: stop signs, traffic lights, speed limits, tailgating laws, etc. Nearly all—if not all—traffic incidents occur because someone is violating or disregarding one or more of these rules, laws, etc.

Now consider the number of times that you have disregarded or violated one of these rules. These are rules that have been designed to **prevent** accidents. These rules are not frivolous. They mostly make sense. What they say is this: "Violate the rule and you'll probably have an accident." Therefore, if you violate the rule, a reasonable and prudent person should EXPECT to have an accident (I mean "incident").

You go through a stop sign. If an accident is the expected result, then is it an accident if you hit someone? Of course not. It's an accident (an unexpected result) if you DON'T hit someone! Are you with me? Good.

So, why do so many people disregard the laws? Why do so many people so often disregard commonsense rules? Answer: Because they get away with it so often—without, as they say, incident. And because they do it so often without incident, there are accidents. If they didn't get away with it as often, they would be more careful and there would be fewer accidents! Thus:

There are so many accidents because there aren't enough accidents.

It really does make perfect sense, doesn't it?

The prescriptive advice, then, is quite obvious. In order to reduce the number of accidents, we must have more accidents.

I warned you that we were talking "deep thinking," didn't I?

Are You Doing Your Part?

You must do your part. I can see the bumper sticker now: "Do your part! Hit someone today!"

The next time someone goes through a stop sign, don't slam on the brakes. Hit him!

The next time some jerk cuts you off, don't swerve into the curb. Smash into her!

And be sure to perform these acts of bravery and self-lessness at times that will cause the most disruption. No sense getting all smashed up at 2 A.M., when there's no one around to get the message. Rush-hour traffic is best.

Every day there must be complete and utter disruption on the roads during rush hour.

The insurance companies will ultimately be eternally grateful to you. You'll be getting a letter that says something like this:

Dear Brave and Selfless Driver:

Global International Assurance and Fidelity Investment Corporation would like to thank you for doing your part in reducing the number of highway accidents by contributing to the Click and Clack "more accidents" policy. As such, you have been enrolled in the "Basically Wonderful Person" Hall of Fame.

As a company—and a corporate world citizen—Global will be forever indebted to you for your selfless acts which will ultimately make the world a better place. It is individuals like yourself—people who think not of their own safety, but for the long-term "good" of humanity—who make it worthwhile for me to get up and go to work each day.

Thank you,

Signed: J. Cheever Loophole (The president, who makes so much money that you can't count that high, of the company that owns all the real estate on the planet.)

PS: Due to the large number of insurance claims, your policy has been canceled, as of yesterday. Have a nice day.

ha ha ha ha ha ha

ha ha ha ha ha ha

ha ha ha ha ha ha

ha ha ha ha ha ha

ha ha ha ha ha ha

ha ha ha ha ha ha

ha ha ha ha ha ha

ha ha ha ha ha ha

ha ha ha ha ha ha

ha ha ha ha ha ha

ha ha ha ha ha ha

ha ha ha ha ha ha

ha ha ha ha ha ha

MUSINGS

Waste

anything . . .

except time.

The Parable of the Panhandler

(Tom)

Introduction: Samson and Delilah

I must have seen the movie *Samson and Delilah* when I was at a very impressionable age. I mean, the audacity of that little vixen to cut Samson's hair, thereby causing him to lose his strength. The sheer audacity! (Or is it "shear"?)

Ever since seeing that movie, I've gone to great lengths to avoid haircuts. I even grew a beard—just in case it counts. (I've had the beard since I was a young lad—in my thirties, that is. I've never shaved it since then. And, since I married my lovely bride after that, she has never seen my naked face! Now doesn't that explain a lot?)

In any event, I eschew haircuts. (I've been dying to use that word, "eschew." It's a word one should not eschew.)

Where was I? Oh, yeah. I eschew haircuts. My kids are

always asking, "Are you going to get a haircut someday?" My wife—the epitome of tact and diplomacy—usually says something like "Perhaps you might want to consider doing something about your hair?" (Someone—I suspect our producer, Doug Berman—actually sneaked out one day and put a bumper sticker on my Dodge Dart that said "I can't AFFORD a haircut.)

Part I: The Panhandler

Panhandler. I looked it up. I know what it means, but I wondered about its derivation. Unfortunately, it's French. Evidently, "panhandle" is French for "the extended forearm," and thus the evolved definition "to stop someone in the street and ask for food or money."

Since learning the derivation, I give a buck to just about anyone who extends his forearm. People reach out to shake my hand, I give them a buck.

Harvard Square is the world headquarters for panhandlers. You can't walk 2 blocks without encountering half a dozen outstretched forearms. Some people get annoyed at these guys, but I figure if I've got a buck and they don't, why not give it to them? And some of them really ought to be rewarded for their creativity. The signs, for example. Some panhandlers are a bit shy, I guess. So, instead of asking, "Spare change?" or "Got a quarter?" or "Help a guy out?" they spend a little time at home and produce literature; a small billboard, actually. "Honest, hardworking vet needs a little help to get back on his feet" or "Ph.D. in Art History. Laid off from Burger King." This is Harvard Square, after all.

But I do draw the line at drunks. If a guy can't even stay sober while he's working (panhandling is working, isn't it?), then I figure he doesn't deserve my buck. So, the drunk I passed every day in the North End never got a buck from me. Not that he didn't try. He always asked the same way: "Got a quarter?" He was terribly unkempt. (I've always wanted to use that word, too. Unkempt.) When I say "unkempt," I mean he was filthy. Long, dirty hair, straggly beard, disgusting clothes. And always drunk. I did feel sorry for him, but it just didn't seem right to help him get even drunker. Day after day, "Got a quarter?" Yeah, I had a quarter, but I wasn't going to give it to him.

Part II: The Denouement

So, one day I'm walking down Hanover Street in the North End. The drunk is there. "Got a quarter?" I keep walking. But this time, as I'm passing him (obviously without responding to his outstretched forearm), he says, "Why don't you shave that beard?"

I'm shocked. I don't turn back, but I'm thinking, *This guy is the most disheveled human I've ever seen, and he's giving ME grooming advice!*

I keep walking, figuring that he's now working on his next potential client. Instead, he's obviously still following me with his eyes, because I get half a block away and—just to add insult to injury—I hear him yelling at me, "AND GET A HAIRCUT!"

True story.

Omean Aspiavodos

Hello, my name is Tom Magliozzi and I'm a recovering bum. I guess I've always been a bum and I always will be. After all, given my education—to quote a famous man—"I coulda been a contender." I mean, many of my fellow graduates are company presidents or otherwise big muck-a-mucks. And what am I? I do a Mickey Mouse radio show and I write silly stuff for our Web site. Sure, I go to my office almost every day, but it's mostly because my wife wants me out of the house. So, basically, I'm a bum.

Actually, I was a real, unadulterated, full-fledged, card-carrying bum for a while. In my bio (earlier in the book) you read the story of my brush with death on my way to work one morning many years ago. (I went straight to my boss's office and quit.)

For the next two years or so, I collected unemployment and hung out in Harvard Square. With the other bums.

I should mention—for those of you who are contemplating bumness—that it has certain advantages. For one, you avoid a lot of expenses and disagreeable activities related to working, like having starched shirts, buying suits, buying lunch for others, and, of course, the work itself.

And, for two, being broke brings out one's creative nature. For example, during my bum days, meals were a problem. Then I discovered Grendel's Den in the Square, which had an all-you-can-eat lunch buffet for 2 bucks (it was 1974). It went from 11 A.M. to 3 P.M. Quite a deal for a bum. But not good enough. So, here's what I did. I'd arrive promptly at 11 and have breakfast (you're way ahead of me, aren't you?). Then, I'd sit and read the paper or a few chapters of a good book (I think those were the Carlos Castañeda days). At about 2:30, I'd do what? Have lunch, of course. After all, it WAS all-you-can-eat from 11 to 3, wasn't it? Two meals, 2 bucks. Quite a deal, even for 1974.

Meeting girls was a problem, too. No water cooler to stand around and make small talk—or, as the Brits would say, chat up the birds. But creativity again came to the rescue. I lived in a complex of several hundred apartments that was well populated with attractive females.

But how to meet them? When my apartment needed painting, I discovered that the owners of the complex would supply the paint, but not the painter. I got my free paint and painted my apartment. Then I thought, "What a great way to supplement my meager unemployment 'income'—paint other people's apartments." And who, pray tell, were these "other people"? They were the attractive females that I had only seen in the elevator. I put an ad in the laundry room. MAX WASSERMAN WILL SUPPLY THE PAINT, AND I'LL PAINT YOUR APARTMENT FOR $50 A ROOM. SEE TOM, APT 6B."

I had to—as they say—beat them off with a stick.

During this time, I also discovered transcendental meditation. I brought flowers, fruit, and 75 hard-earned dollars to the TM center on Garden Street and got my mantra. I meditated each morning (while waiting for Grendel's Den to open). Two interesting things happened that were related to the meditation.

For a while, I was really into it. I'd meditate for hours at a time. Sometimes I wouldn't leave my apartment for days (when not eating at Grendel's, canned sardines were the only menu item; high in protein, low in cost). During one of these meditation marathons that lasted for about two weeks, I finally decided to venture out to the Square. I walked, as I always did. When I got to the Square, I was ambling toward Grendel's. (That is another advantage of being a bum—one ambles. What's the hurry? Ambling allows one to see and feel things that aren't otherwise available to the senses. No one ambles anymore.) Anyway, I was ambling. A woman was walking toward me. I had never seen her before; a complete stranger. As I approached her, she stopped and stared at me. I stopped. She said, "You should come out more often." And she walked on. Explain THAT.

The second curious event: I was meditating. Had been for quite a while. I must have fallen asleep, because I was lying down when I suddenly woke, sat bolt upright, and said the words "Omean Aspiavodos." (I'm guessing at the spelling.

I pronounced it as Ö mee *ahn* As pee *ah* vuh dose.) Then I said, "What? Who's Omean Aspiavodos?"

Since then I have become convinced that Omean Aspiavodos is some sort of "channel" to the world beyond. A mentor, who will someday help me to achieve nirvana. He (or she) has not surfaced since that time. And not for lack of trying on my part.

Who IS Omean Aspiavodos?

POSTSCRIPT:

If you know who Omean Aspiavodos is (hopefully, he's a wise man living in the mountains of Tibet), please write to me c/o Penguin Putnam Inc.

If you ARE Omean Aspiavodos and you were knocking on my door—yelling your name in an attempt to wake me from my sleep to sell me magazine subscriptions—that would be very disappointing. Please don't bother to write. A person needs his dreams.

The Mystic Valley Boys

(Tom)

We play bluegrass. Me on stand-up bass, my brother on guitar, Stanley on mandolin, and Ronny on banjo. When Joe Val died (you may have heard of Joe Val and the New England Blue Grass Boys—the inspiration for our theme song), there was a commemorative concert for him. We were asked to play. (Well, we weren't *really* asked to play. Stanley organized the concert and Stanley asked us to play.)

We rehearsed for weeks.

When our turn came, my brother introduced us with the following: "We are obliged by federal law to issue the following Surgeon General's warning: We suck."

And we do.

And we did.

The following day, the *Boston Globe* published a review of the show. They mentioned us. The reviewer—I think his name is Scott Alarik—said, "Click and Clack, who with a couple of other guys, go by the name of the Mystic Valley Boys, played several numbers and they weren't half bad."

We *"weren't half bad!"*

We were ecstatic. Not half bad! Wow.

We still don't know exactly what that means, but we're still ecstatic.

After all, he didn't say that we suck.

But we do.

And we did.

The Committee on Student Apathy

(Tom)

When my brother was in his second or third senior year at MIT, he was elected president of the NRSA, the Non-Resident Student Association. Members were students who were what? Right. Non-residents. I mean, even if you lived at home, you ought to have a place to hang your hat—so to speak. That place was the NRSA. Somehow the NRSA had become a motley collection of reprobates and goof-offs. Pinball (Pac Man had not yet made its appearance) was the major pastime, and the association awarded a prize each year to the student who had been at the Institute the longest—without having been awarded a degree (of course).

As president of the NRSA, my brother was an ex officio member of the campuswide Committee on Student Apathy.

He mentioned this odd-sounding committee to me one day, and I said, "What does the committee do?"

He says, "I don't know. I've never gone to any of the meetings."

The IMM Syndrome

(Tom)

We Italians like to think of ourselves as tough studs. It's a sham.

The truth is that some people are tough and some just aren't. If you have some vague notion that you're tough, let me give you a "working definition" of tough. My wife is tough. I aren't. She gets it from her father, Pete.

A little background:

My father-in-law, Pete, lives in a big old house in Maine. I discovered to my dismay that the place has no heat. No heat! He and Florence (the infamous mother-in-law) have a wood-burning stove in the kitchen and a couple of fireplaces scattered around other rooms. But on the second floor—there's no heat.

The second floor—the floor where the bedrooms are. The place where you take off your clothes to go to bed.

There's no heat on that floor. The second floor—the floor where the bathroom is; i.e., where you take off ALL your clothes to take a shower. There's no heat on that floor. (I found all this out one weekend when we decided to visit. We don't do that anymore.)

For a southern European like myself, this is inhumane treatment. When I complained about the lack of heat, I was accused of being a wimp. My masculinity was called into question. I overheard words whispered to Joanne like "What were you thinking?"

So, whence does the wood come to feed the various wood-burning stoves and fireplaces? This is Maine. The woods are all around the house, and when Pete wasn't working, he was out in the woods felling trees and cutting them into bite-size pieces.

One cold winter Saturday, Pete is out in the woods felling trees. There is no one else at home. Pete happily fires up his trusty chain saw. ("You don't have a chain saw?" he says to me incredulously one day. No, I don't have a damn chain saw! I only recently got an electric drill! I stopped shaving because I was afraid of the razor blades.) Anyway, he starts to fell his woodstove fodder. Unfortunately, speaking of felling, he drops the chain saw, which—still running—fells [sic] on his leg—almost cutting it off at the knee.

Ouch.

Think about what you'd do in this situation. I mean, after you started to cry. And after you fainted. And after you bled to death. After all that. Think what you'd have done.

What does Pete do? He calmly removes his belt and makes a tourniquet for the affected leg. He then hobbles about a mile back to the house.

Dial 911? Call an ambulance? Call a neighbor for help? No, he's going to drive to the hospital. HE'S GOING TO DRIVE TO THE HOSPITAL!!!

But he can't drive to the hospital dressed like he is. He's filthy. After all, he's been felling trees all morning. He may run into someone he knows. Not in these clothes, he says. So, he removes the tourniquet and hops into the shower, changes his clothes, and drives to the hospital—20 minutes away—where the emergency room doctor sews him up with 40 or 50 stitches.

Does he call in sick the next day? Take a guess.

That's what I call tough.

Coming from this kind of background, you can imagine Joanne's attitude toward other people's pain and suffering. My poor kids never get to take a sick day from school. ("Malaria? It'll go away. Get dressed, the bus is coming.")

Joanne simply cannot abide wimp behavior.

Nor do I get to take a day off from work. ("You're not going to work because you fell off the ladder onto your head? That was yesterday! Get OVER it! Get dressed, the bus is coming.")

But I have a low tolerance for pain and suffering. When I hurt, I hurt. When I'm in pain, I'm in pain. She laughs when I tell her my hair hurts. "How can your hair hurt? Hair has no nerves!" I'm telling you, when I get sick, my hair hurts.

She's been trying to toughen me up for 20 years. It's not working.

Now she has a theory.

She's even come up with a name for it—Italian Male Malaise Syndrome, or IMM for short. She claims that

Italian males—despite the Italian stallion persona they attempt to project—are a bunch of wimps.

So, if you're Italian and you have the misguided notion that you're tough, fuggedaboudit.

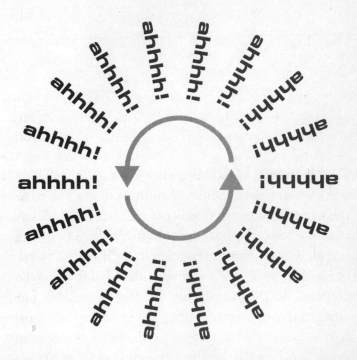

UFOs

(Ray)

My wife watches every UFO show that's on TV, in the hope that one of them will confirm that we've had, or currently have beings from another planet here on Earth. I keep asking her, "What's the matter? Don't you like humanoids?" She just gives me that look. If you're married, you know the look; then she says that I don't have any imagination. Well, I have plenty of imagination, but I simply cannot imagine that any alien beings have visited planet Earth.

First of all, I find it hard to believe that there are alien beings with technology so advanced that it can bring them from star systems light-years away, only to crash and kill them here in the remotest deserts of . . . New Mexico. I can just hear the spaceship flight recorder now: "Gort, Gort, you dummy, fire the retro-rockets. *Crash!*"

In addition, it seems that if they were planning to make a visit the least they could do is send us some advance warning. You shouldn't just "drop in" from another stellar system. Miss Manners would be appalled.

How about something like the radio signal—as primitive as that might be to them—so we could at least have an ambulance waiting. Now those SETI installations, you know the Search for Extra-Terrestrial Intelligence, they've been listening to everything coming from outer space for years. And except for that Jodie Foster movie, which was great science fiction, there's been zero, nada, zip, not a sound. Why? Well, even though I do believe that there are probably other beings out there, there's about a one in a hundred billion chance of them finding us. There are just way too many other planets out there, and furthermore, if they did happen to find us, I don't think they'd even bother to land. We're just too primitive and we have nothing to offer them. If we weren't so primitive, we'd be out finding them. So why so many UFO sightings? Why are people claiming to see all kinds of spaceships, all over the place?

Finally, The Truth.

Well, here's the straight dope on it—according to our crack researcher, Paul Murky of Murky Research and Private Investigations. When World War II ended, the United States came into possession of a lot of inventions that the Third Reich had been working on; things like experimental vehicles, rockets, jet planes, flying wings, God knows what else. Of course, we also came into possession of Wernher von Braun and rocket science.

And, let us not forget that not only were the Germans working on—as we call it in the military—"secret stuff," but we were too. So we had all these experimental aircraft plans, even actual aircraft, and where are you going to test these things? Well, you're certainly not going to test them at Pease Airforce Base in downtown Portsmouth, New Hampshire. You're going to take all these things out to the desert in Nevada or New Mexico or Arizona. You're going to test them out there because, first of all, you expect most of them to crash, and you don't want to kill any innocent people. Of course, if you had to kill innocent people, so be it. But the more important consideration was—if any of them were viable—that you certainly didn't want anyone to see it! It's a secret weapon, duh! And then, of course, the government also figured out that they were going to lose some of these things, and have some spectacular accidents. And who would witness these spectacular accidents? Those few crackpots living in the middle of the desert? Who's going to believe them anyway? No one, because they're crackpots living in the middle of the desert. If they weren't crackpots they wouldn't be living in the middle of the desert.

So that's what's going on, plain and simple. It's government research, secret government research. It's experimental vehicles, it's nothing more than that. There are no little green men. There's no Hanger 18. There's no Hanger 19. There's no nothing. Give up! Take up another hobby, get a life! There's nothing out there that's been in touch with us. Not yet. I think when they do come, we'll know it. They'll land in Washington, DC. Trust me on this.

MEMORIES
are the only
Paradise
from which man
CAN NOT BE DRIVEN

●

—GOETHE

Raising a Kid 101

(Ray)

Twenty-seven years ago, when my wife and I found out that she was pregnant, our doctor insisted that we attend Lamaze birthing classes. It was the "in" thing to do. So we went, and after 8 or 9 2-hour classes, we learned to pant. Yes, pant. Well actually, she learned to pant. I was just the coach. So I got to wear the windbreaker and pace up and down the sidelines and basically call the plays, but essentially, all we learned after 16 hours of classroom instruction was this panting routine.

Now, excuse me, but I think that any woman in the throes of rapid-fire contractions is going to figure out this panting business, birthing classes and coaches notwithstanding.

Yeah, yeah, I know. Millions of women are out there saying, "Oh, yeah? Why don't you try it, wise guy?"

Anyway, after a very long labor, for which the classes never adequately prepared us, my wife gave birth to our first child, a robust, healthy, and handsome (looks like his mother, thank God) baby boy.

After the euphoria subsided, about 10 minutes later, Monique and I looked at each other and simultaneously uttered the same words: "What now?" What are we supposed to do after this? What are we supposed to do for the next 18 years?

Our 16 hours of birthing classes had indeed prepared us for this day, but had also lulled us into believing that this was the hard part, that bringing a newborn into the world was the part of child rearing that necessitated the classes and that the rest would be easy.

But we knew better, and we were scared. So after a few perfunctory lessons in bathing and diaper-changing, the hospital sent us home, all 3 of us. It soon became apparent to all 3 of us that we, the parents, didn't know what the hell we were doing. I remember that first night like it was only 26 years ago. Our little baby, who had been the model of perfection at the hospital, began to cry, and nothing we could do seemed to help. It went on for hours, or so it seemed. In desperation, we tried panting, but to no avail. Fortunately, with the help of family and friends we got through those first few difficult months. I very soon realized that this child-rearing business wasn't easy. And it's the rearing that we really need a course for, not panting during labor.

Throughout my years of parenting, I've always felt a sense of inadequacy. Am I doing too much of this or too little of that? Am I too hard? Am I too easy? And I, like almost everybody else, have had to learn this parenting business on the fly—you know, by trial and error. I guess that most of the experts—you know, the sociologists—would agree that a family's oldest child is subjected to the worst parenting and subsequent kids are the beneficiaries of the early mistakes. This might explain why Tommy is such a wacko, and I, being 12 years younger, am so well adjusted.

But I digress. The point I'm trying to make here is that everyone needs a course on child rearing so we don't make the same mistakes our parents and our grandparents made. Wouldn't it be nice if you could get some real classroom instruction on how to deal with and understand a 2-year-old's temper tantrums? Wouldn't it be great if you knew why your 7-year-old locked herself in the bathroom, or why your 10-year-old tried to drown the cat in the toilet? Wouldn't it be enlightening and helpful to know why your twins decided to paint the hood of your brand-new car—with a rock?

Most of us don't have any idea what to expect from our children as they progress through childhood, and thus we react inappropriately when our kids "misbehave." I can't tell you how many times I've been at the mall and seen a mother screaming at a 2-year-old to "shut up and stop crying." More than a few times I have witnessed a father berate a Little Leaguer in front of 20 teammates for letting a grounder go through his legs. Now if these dopes are behaving like this in public, imagine what's going on in the privacy of their own homes. Yikes!

Stuff like this has been going on for too long, and it needs to be stopped. Child rearing is serious business and needs to be treated as such. If we don't do something, we'll continue to churn out an ever increasing number of wackos and misfits.

The way to change this is through education. Each and every one of us needs to learn how to love and respect our kids and to deal with all the ups and downs of parenting. And we need to learn what it takes to do the job correctly. Here's what I propose.

Every high school senior should be required to study parenting for at least a semester, and you can't get your diploma unless you pass the course. No one does anything the last 3 months of high school anyway, and this would be a great time to teach these essential skills. Prospective parents should be learning parenting and not panting, in my humble opinion. OK, I'll get off my soapbox now. Thanks.

I need to add a little postscript to this Rant and Rave from a personal experience.

While I was writing this rant, the following little drama unfolded in our own household. My wife and I, along with our younger son, Andrew, had decided to go out to dinner one night, and just as we were about to leave, he announces, "I'm not going with you."

I said, "What are you talking about? Your mother and I discussed this with you an hour ago, and you agreed to come with us."

He said, "I'm not going."

"Why not?" I asked.

"I hate you," he answered with finality.

My wife went outside to sit in the car, but I refused to leave. I wanted to listen. I wanted to find out where this hatred came from. He went on to say, "I don't know what it is, Dad, but right now I can't stand the sight of you. Just the thought of looking at your faces and listening to your voices is enough to make me sick, and I know I wouldn't be very good company."

Wow! That was a shocker.

He continued, "I love you more than anything else in the world, but I just can't look at you right now. There's something about you and Mom that's making me sick to my stomach."

So I left him alone. Monique and I went out to dinner by ourselves, and when we got home, everything was fine.

I remember times in my own life when I hated my parents. Everything they said was either stupid or ignorant, or they embarrassed the hell out of me. Looking back on this little incident, I guess I feel fortunate that our son was able to communicate with us what his hormones were obviously doing to his brain, and had it not been for his ability to verbalize what was going on, we might easily have acted inappropriately.

Andrew's behavior that night was just a normal part of growing up, and had he not been able to share with us what he was feeling, we wouldn't have understood it, and we could easily have done something awful. And we were lucky. Andrew's 17 years old. You'd think that after all these years we would have figured this stuff out.

We're learning every day.

A Seductive Plot of Enormous Complexity and Brilliant Subtlety

(Tom)

Little boys play with trucks. Little girls spend much of their young not-so-innocent lives planning to bankrupt their fathers. I speak from experience.

A few years ago, my lovely daughter was married. And I soon became quite destitute. I was appalled at the cost of the wedding, as I'm sure most Fathers of the Bride are. It was absolutely outrageous. As the wedding plans progressed, the costs kept escalating. As any loving father would, I made a desperate attempt to stem the hemorrhaging.

I tried to bribe my daughter. I first offered her $5,000 to run away and send us a postcard. Five large ones, I soon came to realize, was a pittance; an insult, in fact. I upped it to $10,000. No deal. I went to $20,000. Still no deal.

Now, I had always thought that my daughter was some-what intelligent. (God knows she should be, after all that tuition money for private schools and colleges.) And indeed, she IS intelligent. What I had failed to consider was that being a daughter also made her a female. In retrospect, I realize that my attempts at bribery—feeble though they may have been—were destined to fail at any amount. I now realize that had I been able to raise the offer to 100 grand (yeah, right), I would still have had no deal.

I've wondered why. Now, I think I know. If you have a married daughter, you, too, may already know. If you have a yet unmarried daughter, pay close attention. There are two possible reasons.

The Marital-Industrial Complex

One factor is the conspiracy known as the Marital-Industrial Complex—that coalition of hotels, wedding gown manufacturers, purveyors of silverware, bone china, jewelry, appliances, and all manner of useless items that hang on walls.

Somehow this coalition has managed to brainwash an entire country—if not an entire planet—of otherwise intelligent females into believing that they cannot get married without (their fathers) hosting a Grand Ball for everyone the bride has ever met, anyone remotely associated with everyone she's ever met, and in some cases, strangers she's bumped into on the subway (plus, of course, the groom's immediate family; no friends).

One must certainly give credit to the coalition for a feat of such overwhelming magnitude and complexity. Certainly multinational corporations and governments would have more than a passing interest in the techniques used to accomplish such a massive plot of deception and propaganda.

But all the efforts of the Marital-Industrial Complex would come to naught were there not in place an underlying Collective Consciousness that I call . . .

The Cinderella Syndrome

Throwing a party for anyone your daughter has ever met is one thing. But when it comes to pomp and splendor, a wedding is in a class by itself. A rajah would be proud to be the host. How, pray tell, have we reached this sad (and incredibly expensive) state of affairs? Partly, it is because fathers love their daughters and will do almost anything to spare them shame and disappointment. And, unfortunately, meeting their expectations requires the proverbial king's ransom.

The brainwashing process begins almost at birth. As soon as the child is barely able to understand, the process has taken hold. (Words are not required; pictures are worth thousands of words. I just made that up. It's good isn't it? A picture is worth a thousand words. I like it.)

It begins with the story of Cinderella, a seductive tale of enormous power. In it, a girl/woman, persecuted by her evil stepsisters and stepmother, attains the Holy Grail of Womandom: She marries Prince Charming (whom she weds dressed in a magnificent sequined flowing gown—having been chauffeured to the celebration in a carriage drawn by several dozen Budweiser Clydesdale horses).

This tale is told to unsuspecting little girls—sometimes by

their even more unsuspecting fathers. It is told and told again. The sweet innocent daughters are spellbound. As they grow, other players contribute to the plot. Disney Enterprises takes up the baton for a decade or so with similar tales; different, yet all the same. A plain girl marries a prince. After Disney it is romance novels, the media, and all manner of coconspirators.

Thus the imagery has decades to build to proportions beyond belief (a man's belief, that is).

For example, this past year, my other lovely (younger, yet unmarried) daughter attended approximately 45 bat mitzvahs (the female counterpart of the bar mitzvah—OK, it only seemed like 45). There was one a week for about a year—each, of course, requiring a new outfit. For one of them, the invitation read:

Time: Midnight to dawn
Place: The Taj Mahal
Dress: Dress to kill

Now, I realize that there is religious significance to this rite of passage to adulthood, but the extravagance does indeed give one pause.

Most of these "rites" were far more elaborate than any wedding I have ever attended. The consequence of this splendor and extravagance is continuous reinforcement of the Cinderella Syndrome—while at the same time increasing the wedding expectations to higher and higher levels of unattainable grandeur. (As an example of the heights to which these expectations can be driven, my older daughter attended the wedding of one of her college classmates at which the Ohio State University marching band performed for the guests. Enough said.)

Nature vs. Nurture—and a Prescription

I began this little rant with the observation that as children—almost from birth—boys play with trucks and girls plot to bankrupt their fathers. Is it nature or nurture? That is, does our culture contribute strongly to this profound difference in play among boys and girls? If so, then perhaps we have an opportunity to protect ourselves from the financial debacle to which we fathers of daughters are ineluctably destined.

I could attempt to convince you that nurture plays a strong role here. But it does not. It is 100% nature. There is not a single thing we can do about it. It's as old as time. We are doomed.

But must we be willing partners in our own financial demise? I think not.

I have peered ahead at my next life, and I have seen my defense.

Picture it, if you will. My beautiful, loving, soft, cuddly daughter climbs up on my lap in her pink Doctor Dentons. She kisses me on the cheek and hugs me with all the strength her small body can muster. I am overwhelmed with love.

"Daddy, Daddy, please read me the Cinderella story again."

"Oh, shut up. Go play with a truck."

Hell, it's worth a try.

NEVER LEND MONEY TO A FRIEND OR RELATIVE

AMNESIA

it causes

OR RELATIVE

NEVER LEND MONEY TO A FRIEND

The Theory of Abstract Cooking

(Tom)

I know the following piece of information is going to break the hearts of millions of women, but it must be said.

My brother and I are happily married. (No, not to each other.)

It so happens that Joanne (my wife) and Monique (you figure it out), though related only by marriage (Monique refers to herself as "Tom's sister-in-law by marriage"), have some interesting characteristics in common. For example, they frequently—without prior communication—dress alike. Or they each decide to get a haircut and . . . voila . . . same style. Buy a new pocketbook? Same one. These are just little things and could even be considered mere coincidences. However, each of them has developed—quite independently—a very interesting . . . shall we call it an attitude? . . . about cooking.

I'll tell you about their ideas and you decide if it's coincidence (or conspiracy).

First, Joanne

I only recently discovered that Joanne has quite an unusual philosophy regarding cooking. She subscribes to many cooking magazines (*Gourmet* is the only one I happen to remember, but there are others). In addition, she has four or five shelves of what appear to be very expensive cookbooks. When a new issue of one of the magazines arrives, she devours (you should pardon the expression) its contents.

From all this reading, she has become extraordinarily well versed in the art of cooking. She can trade exotic recipes with the best of them. I recall frequent discussions with the food editor for the *Boston Globe,* who happens to be a friend of hers (interesting in itself). They use vocabulary with which I am quite unfamiliar. Words like "shirr," "reserve," "caramelize," among others that propriety does not allow me to mention in a family book of this kind.

Here's the interesting part. Despite Joanne's in-depth knowledge, and her seemingly unceasing efforts at culinary knowledge, every week we have the same six meals for dinner (we go out to dinner on Friday nights).

Clearly, she knows **how** to prepare more than these basic meals, but she has stuck with the 6 "20-minute gourmet miracles," as she calls them. Where are the exotic recipes?

Then it hit me. She had—perhaps inadvertently—invented a new discipline: **abstract cooking!**

What a concept! Knowledge and expertise without the work! Knowledge in its purest form. Knowledge for its own sake.

Think about the possibilities:

Abstract nuclear engineering: knowledge and expertise without the carnage.

Abstract auto repair: knowledge and expertise without the scraped knuckles (sounds like an idea for a radio show).

I confronted her with this revelation one night as we sat in a fancy restaurant. I had ordered coquilles St. Jacques; it was fantastic. She began to explain the ingredients and the steps in the preparation of said coquilles. I said, incredulously, "You know how to make this?"

"Of course"

"Then why don't you ever make it?"

She thought for a minute, then said, "Well, I suppose one could say that it's based on economic theory. For example, Adam Smith's *Wealth of Nations,*" she said. "Surely you've read it."

"Hasn't everyone?"

"Well, then, you surely remember the concept of the division of labor?"

"Yeah, the guys making pins. So?"

"So, think about it. The restaurant is all set up to make these exotic meals. The cooking is done by one person; the serving, by another; cleanup by another. All expert at what they do. Division of labor. The epitome of efficiency. If I did it, I'd have to do everything. And I'd be terribly inefficient at it. So, I leave it to them."

I was flabbergasted. But she wasn't finished.

"And then there's the issue of economies of scale," she went on. "If the restaurant makes it, they're going to make dozens of them in an evening; maybe more. If I make it, I make it for you and me. They have economies in buying the stuff, economies in the labor. Don't you get it?"

No, I didn't get it. And it was clear I wasn't going to get coquilles St. Jacques at home either. I'd call that a rather interesting perspective, wouldn't you?

I think Monique's perspective is equally interesting. And, to my knowledge, developed completely independently— i.e., without collusion with Joanne. I think.

Monique's Revelation

A few years ago, Raymond and Monique bought a house. It was pretty nice. Except that Monique thought the kitchen was too small. (Raymond tried to convince her to paint a picture of a picture window on the kitchen wall. She didn't go for it, but I thought it was a rather clever solution.)

So, they commissioned a contractor to perform what I later found out was known in the trade as a "bump-out."

The bump-out, I came to learn, refers to the fact that although a house may appear large enough (at least to all males), it simply isn't—to nearly all females. So you "bump out" by tearing down an outside wall and adding a room, the new room or extension of an existing room being called, appropriately, "the bump-out." In this case, the new room was an extension of the old kitchen. The old kitchen, I might add, had been considered to be of adequate size by the original designer of the house as well as generations of previous owners. Nonetheless, the kitchen was deemed—by Monique—as inadequate, and the bump-out became a fait-accompli.

Now, this is neither the time nor the place to discuss life with a contractor. Nor is it appropriate here to discuss the parallel universe to which contractors suddenly and inexplicably disappear. Particularly at a time when you have a house with only three walls. No, this is not the time to discuss these issues because, as it turned out, an even more interesting issue emerged.

The new kitchen was wonderful. Spacious and modern in all respects. With every modern convenience from the nuclear fridge to laser light shows, monolithic countertops, and walk-in microwave oven (OK, I'm exaggerating). And, of course, all new. Brand-new. Pristine.

It was shortly after completion of the project—on a par with the construction of the Panama Canal, I might add—that my brother discovered Monique's rather interesting point of view regarding the "new kitchen." Raymond noticed that Monique wasn't cooking anymore. Every night was take-out or go out. When he confronted Monique with his observation by asking her why she wasn't cooking in the new kitchen, she answered, **"What. And make a mess?"**

Yes, Monique had observed—quite correctly, of course—that cooking in her pristine kitchen made a mess!

How right she was. Cooking does indeed make a mess. Raymond tried to remain calm, but he did inquire why she hadn't told him about this rather important and interesting point of view before they had put themselves into hock for 50 large ones. Her answer was "I just thought of it."

What Are the Chances?

The comedian Steven Wright tells a great story. Two guys are talking about sports. The older guy mentions Lou Gehrig, whom the younger guy has never heard of. The older guy says, "You know. He's the guy who died of Lou Gehrig's disease." The younger guy says, "Wow, what are the chances of that?"

I'm having the same thoughts about Joanne and Monique. I mean, they both arrive—by different routes, I admit—at a point that results in their doing no cooking.

Conspiracy? Collusion? Duplicity?

Or simply coincidence?

A Taxonomy of Humankind

(Tom)

I love theories, don't you? My wife is the master of theories (mistress of theories?). She has a theory about everything. I'll say something like "Gee, isn't it funny how John reacted to what I said?" And she'll say, "Well, I think that people who **(1)** have a tendency to **(2)** because **(3)** ."

(1) Select one of the following:

Hate their mothers
Are ambidextrous
Drive a Volvo
Pick their noses.

(2) Select one of the following:

> Sleep late
> Grow tomatoes
> Live in sin
> Eat garlic.

(3) Select one of the following:

> They have a repressed libido gland.
> Their left-brain chemistry has too high a pH.
> Their siblings stuffed cabbage up their noses when they
>   were kids.
> They're Italian, and all Italians do that.

And I say, "Wow!"

And she says, "I don't know. It's just a theory."

But every single one of her innocent-sounding little observations has embedded in it the topic for a doctoral dissertation. So, if you're at the dissertation phase of your doctoral program and you need a topic, drop her a note. It doesn't matter what your major is—or even if she's ever heard of it. The more obscure, the better.

I myself have a theory occasionally. Here's one that I came up with while drinking espresso at the Caffé Paradiso—the one in Harvard Square.

ASIDE: There are several Caffé Paradisi in the Boston area. Each has its own character and therefore serves a different purpose in my life. For example, the one in the North

End—the Italian enclave of Boston—is the one where I drink espresso and look at people. I don't think of much of anything. I just look. Once in a while, I may say something deep and insightful, like "hmmm." Other times, I just watch the meter maids giving tickets to the double parkers. Or I watch the mafioso wanna-bes across the street sitting in their Cadillac convertibles. In other words, I just survey the passing scene—as they say.

But the Caffé Paradiso in The Square is for pondering. I do sit and look at people, but frequently I become encumbered by the thought process. Here's what came out one day last summer. (I made notes on a napkin which I still have.)

The Genesis of a Theory

It's difficult to say exactly what triggered the train of thought, but it was something like this. I was sitting at a sidewalk table, looking at people walking by. (To the unsuspecting, I probably looked like I was doing here what I do at the Caffé Paradiso in the North End. Au contraire, piston puss. There I look. Here I ponder.) As I looked at the faces of passersby, I realized that I had some strange kind of "kinship" with some of them. If you listen to our radio show, you may have heard me say after a call, "I'd like to have coffee with that guy."

The same thing was happening that day at the Caffé Paradiso. Someone would walk by and I'd say, "Yup. Coffee." Next person, I'd say "Nope. Not interested." My right brain was in overdrive. I.e., I had no idea what the determining factor(s) was/were in my decision. It was just Yup or Nope. One thing I did notice, though, was that there was no pattern to the Yups and Nopes. Both groups contained males, females, young, old, kids, all ethnic and racial groups, well-dressed dowagers and bums.

Then I got it. It was the eyes. Something in the eyes of some of the people passing by was telling me that he or she and I were simpatico. It was more than simpatico. It was deeper. Not just that we could like each other, but that we were of one mind. We had the same values. And we wouldn't have to talk about much because we'd both "know." Wow! This was heavy.

I realized that I sort of knew this already. Have you ever walked down the street and had your eyes meet those of a person walking toward you? And spontaneously you say, "How ya doin'?" And s/he says, "How ya doin'?" And you both continue walking. Happens to me all the time. The eyes. The eyes are indeed the windows to the soul.

Then, my left brain kicked in. I started counting the Yups and Nopes. (That's what left brainers are good at. Stuff like counting.) Then I started estimating the *degree* of Yupness and Nopeness. (Left brainers are good at things like estimating.) So, as someone walked by, I'd find myself saying things like "Coffee? Absolutely." Or "Hmmm, maybe." Or "No way."

Here's what I came up with. The Yups were undeniable and unmistakable. When I saw one of "my" people, I had no trouble identifying him or her. But beyond that, I was able to identify 6 degrees of "no" ranging from "hmm—maybe" to "no way." These 6 categories plus the category of "Yup" led me to:

The Taxonomy of Humankind

It's this:

There exist on the planet only 7 types of people. They may appear to have nothing in common, for each category contains all races, colors, and creeds—as they used to say. Fat, thin, old, young, speaking any language or no language at all. But in their souls the people in each category are the same.

Assuming an even distribution, let's see: 6 billion of us on the planet, divided by 7 categories = about 850 million. Which means we each have a close kinship with 849,999,999 other people. Then there's the group on either side of your group—that's another (2 x 850,000,000 =) 1.7 billion that you can probably get along with. And of course the remainder—about 3.5 billion (including the 850 million at the opposite end of the spectrum from you—that you'd probably detest if they got anywhere near you. (I believe lawyers, insurance salesmen, used car dealers, and stockbrokers are in this group. For me, that is. To other such people, they're soul brothers.)

Now I ask you, is this a dissertation topic, or what?

I've purposely left a few things to be looked into. (Otherwise, it wouldn't be research, now would it? It would be—I think it's called, uh, plagiarism.)

For your dissertation proposal, I'd talk about:

1. Descriptions of each of the 7 groups, including at least psychological characteristics—and anything else you can think of. I'd include photos of eyes. And make sure that your dissertation committee includes at least one person from the Art History department (to comment on the eyes). In fact, maybe you shouldn't use photos. Why not eyes from great works of art? Maybe you pose this question: Are those two people in *American Gothic* married to each other? Should they be? I love it. Then, of course, there's the *Mona Lisa*. And John Singer Sargent's portraits could keep you busy for months. But I've given you too many ideas already. Think for yourself.

2. Name each group. This should be the most fun. I've actually started on this. I've named the group with whom I have the least empathy the Evil Ones. At the other extreme are the Sweet, Gentle, Kind, Awesome, Generous Folk. I'm in this group. The names are extremely important. And of course they will determine the success or failure of your dissertation defense. No good names, no Ph.D.

3. Count them. I've assumed equal numbers of each, but what the hell do I know? Remember, I was just sitting there drinking coffee. Pondering. Musing.

I can see it all now. Based on the results of this research, we'll divide the earth into 7 parts—sizes to be determined by the numbers in each category. Then we ship all members of a category to an appropriate geographic area. I can almost hear you saying, "Boy, that's going to cause trouble. Who gets to choose the areas?" Oh, ye of little faith. There will be no trouble. Step 1 above will, I am sure, include climatic preferences, which will vary dramatically by group membership. Part of the strife in the world today is that these 7 groups have been accidentally and mistakenly "assigned" within what we call "countries." Thus, within any country there exist all 7 groups attempting to coexist. But it's hopeless. It explains all civil wars, doesn't it? And it also explains all other wars. Once everyone is "reassigned" based on eyes, no one will want what someone else has. He'll have what he wants and they'll have what they want. (I admit I am having a little trouble explaining Adolf Hitler.)

P.S. I just received my assignment papers. Seems I'm heading off to Hawaii with my group. I heard that my ex-wives will be somewhere in Siberia. They must be a little short of ice up there.

Progress Run Amok: A Parlor Game for the New Millennium

(Tom)

"Your call is important to us . . .

"Please stay on the line for our automated answering system."

If my call were important to them, wouldn't they answer the %^*)@ phone? Is this progress?

Or is this progress run amok?

It occurred to me the other day that just about all progress is running amok (if "running amok" means "out of control"—which I think it does , but I'm too damn lazy to go look it up). Anyway, think about this, if you will . . .

It seems to me that "progress" occurs in the following way: Some person (maybe a geek) invents something—or thinks up something. Someone (the same person—or usually someone else; we call this someone else an entrepreneur or developer, or maybe exploiter?) decides that it represents a way to make money. And off we go, helter-skelter, in on some new wacko direction—like a machine telling you that your call is so important to them that they won't even bother to answer the phone!

Voila, progress!

Perhaps there should be a third person in the loop. Someone who gets to say, "Whoa, fellas. Is this a good idea for the world? Let's think about it a bit. Where is this invention/discovery/opportunity going to take us?"

What if you were that person—a Philosopher-King or Philosopher-Queen, so to speak?

Some quiet evening when you have a few friends over for coffee (and there's no football game on the tube—or, better yet, if there IS a stupid game on the tube), here's a little game you might want to play. The name of the game is: **Your Call Is Important to Us . . . .**

Here's how it goes (feel free to make up your own rules about how to score points, etc.). The object of the game is to be the first couple in the assembled group to get a divorce. A divorce counts for 10 points, separation is 6 points . . . . Well, you get the idea.

The first player (chosen any damn way you want; what do I care who goes first? Maybe you'll spend most of the evening arguing about how to decide who goes first. Fine.) is the "Philosopher-King/-Queen." S/he selects a card from the Category Deck, which contains categories like Transportation, Communications, Medicine, etc.

Let's look at the first category, Transportation. (Why did I put Transportation first? I really don't know. It was completely arbitrary. But just to prove how wonderfully powerful this game is, my first wife asked me that same question. I said my *first* wife.)

The Philosopher-Queen/-King looks at the category card, reads it to the group, and after careful thought, announces his/her selection to the group. In this case, the category would be Transportation, and the choices are:

TRANSPORTATION

—Feet
—Horse/elephant/etc.
—Bicycle
—Train
—Automobile
—Piston-engine plane
—Jet plane
—No limit

The selection is based on this premise: If you WERE that Philosopher-King/-Queen, (PK or PQ for short) where would you have stopped progress in each of the categories? Feel free to use all the hindsight/foresight/retrospect at your disposal; i.e., knowing what you know now, where would you have said, "Whoa, fellas. Is this a good idea for the world?"

Isn't this great?

We play this game around my house all the time (I've been a winner 3 times now). Below is a little exchange that occurred recently in the Transportation category.

Here are the players:

PK (Philosopher-King)
PKW (Philosopher-King's Wife).

PK: I would have stopped at the train. I grant you that a train wouldn't have gotten us to the moon, but who cares? Trains and boats can get you anywhere on the globe. Sure, it takes a long time. But it takes a long time because it's far! It's supposed to take a long time to go far. If it wasn't supposed to, God would have made the earth smaller.

PKW: [ASIDE: Notice she's the first to jump in.] Oh, stop it! What are you talking about? You're just a crazy old man—in love with the past. Jet planes took us to our honeymoon in Hawaii, didn't they? And besides, how would we be able to visit my mother in Topeka without planes?

PK: [silence; smirk. Can you read his mind? Did you hear "Duh" or "I rest my case?" So did I.]

NOTE: PK now lives in Bermuda. No one knows where PKW is. When last heard from she was selling medicinal herbs door-to-door.

You get the idea. Here are a few more categories to play with. I know a couple of good lawyers. Let me know if (I mean **when**) you want their phone numbers.

COMMUNICATIONS

—Smoke signals
—Telegraph
—Telephone
—Radio
—Television
—Cellular phone

—Internet
—No limit

ENERGY

—Fire
—Fossil-fuel steam power (but not electricity)
—Electricity (fossil-fuel)
—Electricity (nuclear power but not nuclear bombs; see Weaponry)
—No limit

WEAPONRY

—Sticks/clubs
—Bows and arrows
—Muskets/pistols (single-shot)
—Repeating rifles/pistols
—Missiles
—Nuclear bombs
—No limit

MEDICINE

—Twigs/barks/herbs and leeches (includes aspirin)
—X-rays
—Penicillin
—All other antibiotics and medicines beyond penicillin (around 1945)
—Organ transplants
—No limit

MARKETING/MERCHANDISING:

—Barter between individuals
—Marketplaces like the agora
—Neighborhood "mom and pop" stores
—Shopping malls
—E-commerce
—No limit

EDUCATION

—Apprenticeships (formal and informal)
—Home schooling
—Little red schoolhouses (teaching readin', writin', and 'rithmetic)
—Universities and colleges as they exist in the U.S. now
—Internet "schools" and/or courses
—No limit

ECONOMICS

—Barter/exchange using products and one's time
—Money of some kind
—Credit cards
—Ownership of businesses by individuals or very small groups (say 6 people)
—Absentee ownership on a grand scale (i.e., the NYSE)
—No limit

Have fun. Don't forget to ask for the lawyers' phone numbers.

RANTS

It is the lazy man who works the hardest.

It is the stingy man who spends the most.

It is the stingy man who spends the most.

It is the lazy man who works the hardest.

It is the lazy man who works the hardest.

It is the stingy man who spends the most.

It is the stingy man who spends the most.

It is the lazy man who works the hardest.

It is the lazy man who works the hardest.

It is the stingy man who spends the most.

It is the stingy man who spends the most.

It is the lazy man who works the hardest.

It is the lazy man who works the hardest.

It is the stingy man who spends the most.

It is the stingy man who spends the most.

It is the lazy man who works the hardest.

It is the lazy man who works the hardest.

It is the stingy man who spends the most.

The Penal Principle

(Tom)

There I was. Just musing, as I am wont to do. And I mused this. . . .

The way that we "punish" criminals has never made any sense to me. We build expensive facilities in which to incarcerate them. Various sources estimate that a prisoner costs us $30,000 to $50,000 a year. (Yes, it costs *us*. You and me.)

Now let me get this straight. These criminals are people who have said, "I don't want to subscribe to the rules that this society has set up. I want to operate by my own rules. I happen to think it's OK for me to rob, plunder, rape, murder, and whatever else. Catch me if you can." So, we catch them. Then what? Then we pay $30,000 to $50,000 to put them away for a short time in the hope that they'll be dissuaded from doing this again. They aren't dissuaded. They already told us that they don't like our rules. Locking them up for 5, 10, or 50 years doesn't make them like the rules any better. Recidivism rates are very high.

And we pay several times. The $50,000 it takes to keep them away from society for a year is just the beginning. The fact that they've done whatever they've done has lots of other costs. Insurance, for one. All of us pay for insurance to help defray the cost of crime when it strikes us. And not just our own insurance. Every product or service we spend money for has in it an additional cost because of the insurance that the provider had to buy. And money doesn't go just to the insurance companies. All those plainclothes people skulking around Kmart have to get paid. So you buy a pair of shorts and you pay some percentage for the "crime tax"—insurance, guards, shoplifting losses. Then they get caught and they want us to pay again? Why should we pay anything? Just what are we paying for anyway? A year or 2 (or 20) of freedom from that particular criminal? When there are so many to take his place that we don't even know he's gone?

Here's my idea. Since these sociopaths have come right out and stated that they don't like the society that the rest of us have devised (and there *are* more of us than there are of them—at least, so far), why do we allow them to live in it? Why not give them their own society to live in? They deserve each other, don't they? Some would say that the prisons are that society. But *we* build the prisons for them. *We* run them. *We* supply the food, the TVs, the weight room, the heat and light and laundry. Why us? Why are *we* obliged to care for criminals? "Society" has basically said, "Here are the rules that we all agree to follow if we're going to live together." The criminals say, "We don't like the rules." Isn't the obvious response "Fine. Go somewhere else, and make your own society"?

Now I'm not saying that prison is a day at the beach, but it's surely way too good. Why not this: Why not choose an impenetrable location? One that can be easily guarded. Preferably one that has *no* amenities. A jungle, perhaps. The rationale is simple. If you don't want to live here, live there. I can hear the "inhabitants" already: "But there's no food! No TV! No nuthin'! I can't even get in touch with the ACLU!"

Well isn't *that* just too bad? You did say you didn't want to live here, didn't you?

This has all the attributes of a great idea:

1. It solves the problem.
2. It's simple.
3. It's much less expensive than the current solution.
4. And it's not new.

You've probably already recognized this idea. It's Devil's Island. It was the idea behind Australia—but Australia was far too good a place to "give away" to the scum of the earth. So was Devil's Island, for that matter. I personally like Siberia. Or Montana. Someplace that nobody wants. We give it to them and they fend for themselves.

Think about the advantages.

1. All the criminals of the world will be together. If they figure out how to eat, they eat. If they decide to steal from someone else, great. If they decide to kill someone to take his food, excellent. What could be better?

2. The only costs are those of transporting the prisoners to the "island" and protecting against their escape. And it's so simple to guard. We ring the island with battleships. There is no contact with the inhabitants and so no way for unscrupulous guards to make deals, sell dope, or get hurt, for that matter. Anything in the water surrounding the island gets blown to bits. Period. Is it harsh? Didn't *they* tell *us* that they didn't agree with our rules? And weren't we nice enough to provide them with a venue for making their own?

3. Think of the social experiment (not entirely new: *Lord of the Flies*, *Gilligan's Island*). This'll keep the sociologists busy for centuries. Of course, if they go there to write Ph.D. dissertations, they can never leave. Nobody leaves!

4. The American Civil Liberties Union will be busy for centuries, too. Our answer to them will always be the same: "Rave on!"

The tree huggers of the world will, of course, think of a "compromise." For example, this may be OK for hardened criminals, but shoplifting? Come on. How about a less harsh arrangement for minor crimes? Sure, I'll go for that. But all hardened repeaters go to "the island." (Actually, "the rock" has a really nice ring to it, no?)

The reason that prisons aren't a deterrent is that they're too easy. Crime is destroying the country, if not the world. Surely it does not take a rocket scientist to realize this. In a few years, there could be *no* crime. Think about that. No crime. You could walk down any street at any time of day or night. You could leave your doors unlocked. You could pick up hitchhikers again. Your kids could walk to the corner store without getting caught in cross fire. Smith and Wesson would be out of business.

Then we'd have the time to work on the real problems of the world—hunger, disease, and devising a plan to get rid of the jerks in Hollywood who make Rambo movies.

A Bronx Tale—
Sort Of

(Ray)

We grew up in a pretty interesting neighborhood of Our Fair City; and in an area where there were only a handful of streets, we had...ready for this? Two barbershops, a dry cleaner, three candy stores, three bakeries, two stores where you could buy chickens, dead or alive. (To this day, the sign outside one of these chicken stores says Live Chickens—Fresh Killed. I always wondered about this sign. If they were fresh killed, how could they also be live? If they had both, why would you want a live chicken?) We also had a gas station and an accountant. (Why an accountant? you might ask. Read on, my friend.)

One of my most vivid memories of this quaint neighborhood was the barbershop. When I was just a wee lad, my father would take me to Attilio's Tonsorial Emporium (one chair, plenty of waiting). I'd sit in the chair and in the time span of one haircut, the phone would ring 15 or 20 times. Each time, Attilio would disappear into the back room to answer it. In less than a minute he'd be back. I never really knew what was going on, but I knew he was doing something more than just cutting hair. It was much later that I learned Attilio was booking numbers. As were the chicken stores, the three bakeries, the dry cleaner, and the accountant. If you wanted to play a number, you could go to any one of these stores, and do so.

Even our sainted grandmother would occasionally wager a few pennies—yes, pennies—and amazingly, when she needed something like a new pair of shoes or a winter coat, she'd always manage to win $40 or $50, and she'd be all set for another year. Pretty good, huh?

Now everyone knew it was illegal. Of course it was illegal, but it wasn't really hurting anyone; and in our neighborhood, as I'm sure was the case in many other neighborhoods around the country, they even had a kind of support group for people whose gambling habit got out of hand. You know, kind of like Gamblers Anonymous; except in our neighborhood it consisted of Rocko and Vito, who—if you were behind on your gambling debts—would hang a beating on you. A surer cure has yet to be found.

Despite its illegality, this innocent gambling did add a dimension of excitement and intrigue to people's lives. Sure, every once in a while the cops, many of whom had played a number the day before, would raid some bookie joint and haul a few people off to jail, but the next day they were out and everyone knew it was a joke. Life was good. And there was very little real crime in that neighborhood; or in any neighborhood, for that matter. And, although the official unemployment rates may have been high, most everyone was—shall we say—"gainfully employed."

Let us not forget that there had to be an "organization" behind all this gambling. Bets had to be covered, and money had to be transferred from one place to another, thus providing jobs for the many. And let us not forget Rocko and Vito, the "support group" for inveterate gamblers who were unable to make payments on time. In addition, there were various levels of "management"; one could work his way up from a bag man to higher positions of authority (lieutenants, I think they were called). Thus, many people who were otherwise unemployable were kept busy at a kind of gainful activity. And, except for the few occasions when someone was unable to keep up with his payments—and the "support group" had to step in—no one got hurt.

Then the government stepped in. The government figured out that this numbers business was making good money. And they weren't getting a cut. Sure, the government was missing out on its taxes on revenues and winnings, but there was more. What they really wanted was the profits.

If You Can't Join Them, Beat Them.

So our self-righteous legislators came up with a brilliant plan. Obviously the government had to get its share. So how did they do it? By making it legal to play the numbers, via the lottery, thus putting the bookies out of business.

Today you can go to practically any store, and without skulking around in the shadows, you can buy a lottery ticket. Clearly the state governments have taken over the numbers racket, and because they have the power of advertising behind them, they've taken it out of the dark corners and brought it out into the open. They made it legitimate. They made it OK. They've even glamorized it; and in so doing, they have encouraged more and more people to play than ever before. They've also taken away people's savings, and worst of all, they've undermined the work ethic in this country by making people think they can get rich by making a bet. And that's terrible.

But far more important, the government has interfered with the beauty and efficiency of low-level (pretty much), victimless criminal activity.

As we know, every society—and I mean every society— has its criminal element. Some have more than others, but even the ones that we believe are on the up-and-up—you know, the Goody Two-shoes folks—have their criminal element, too. (Do you have money in a numbered Swiss bank account?)

But what troubles me the most is that governmental greed—in its effort to remove this component of the criminal world—has forced these people to move up a rung or two on the ladder of crime. I mean, let's face it, these guys were only booking numbers. All right, they were doing something illegal, but they weren't doing anything terribly bad. And they most certainly weren't doing anything worse than the legalized lotteries are doing now. But by driving these petty criminals out of business, the government has forced them to engage in other forms of criminal activity that are much more harmful to society.

I can just see it. A couple of bookies get put out of business because the legalized state lottery has come into being. They have the following discussion:

"So, Bruno, what you gonna do now?"

"Oh, geez, I don't know. I thought I'd build on my financial skills. Maybe go to Harvard for an MBA, sumthin' like that. How 'bout you, Lefty?"

"I don't know. I been sorta thinkin' 'bout medicine, maybe dermatology. The hours are good, the money ain't too bad."

Yeah, right.

So now we have these bookies who weren't hurting (almost) anybody, and maybe, it could be argued, were doing a service to the community, suddenly unable to make an honest living—so to speak. So where did they go? They were forced by circumstances to use their skills in other activities—like selling guns and drugs. And that's the shame of it, and that's why I hate the lottery. We should abolish it, and let the bookies go back into business. It's a foolproof way to reduce real crime and put some of our friends and family members back to work. In my humble opinion.

Help Us Overthrow the Tall/Short Mafia

(Ray)

Our New Year's resolution for this coming year is going to involve Starbucks Coffee.

Now as good as their coffee is, they have unnecessarily complicated my life, and probably everyone else's life, too. I'm not even going to deal with the fact that they make you choose between a million different kinds of coffee, like decaf, macchiato, americano, skinny, ice, mocha, latte, schmatte, and all that stuff. We'll deal with that problem another time.

Today, I want to deal with their ridiculous size-related nomenclature. And I want to tell you what *we* can do to wipe it off the face of the earth. Keep reading, because this "resolution" includes an exciting call to action that we can *all* participate in.

Remember the old days, when you asked for a cup of coffee and someone would say "Large or small?" Well, apparently "large" and "small" weren't good enough for Starbucks. Noooooo. So they come out with "short" and "tall." That's pretentious, but it's not the end of the world. If it had stopped there, I wouldn't be asking the entire Car Talk Nation to rise up and join me in my Coffee Action today.

So what went wrong? Well, suddenly "tall" became "medium." So if you ask for a "tall," you get a "medium." Well, I didn't want a "medium." I wanted *tall*! Tall is what!? *Big*! *Tall*! Right??

It turns out they've introduced a new size…above "tall." "Grande!" So now "grande" is large, "tall" is medium, and "short" is small. You follow me?

Then they add a whole other group of drinks, for which there is an even *larger* size than "grande." Now, in some drink categories, you can get a "venti"! That's apparently Italian for "humongous." And to make matters worse, you can't get a "short" in that category, so "tall" becomes "small!" I went in and asked for a "tall," and I got the smallest thing on the menu! And I'm sick of it!!! Sick, I say!

So for the last three months, every time I go into one of their stores, I end up having a fight with the poor guy with the nose ring behind the counter. I say "I want a small iced cappuccino," and the guy says, "You mean tall?" "*No, I don't mean tall*! I said small, and I mean small!" I duke it out with the guy while 10 people behind me are yelling and screaming to have me physically ejected from the store. Then I have to go down the street to Dunkin Donuts— where they still understand the words "large" and "small."

So here's my resolution, and I hope everyone reading this

today will join me in this worthwhile project. I'm going to walk into Starbucks from now on and I'm going to refuse to play their game. I'm going to refuse to use their obtuse nomenclature.

From now on, I'm going to walk up to the counter and say, "Gimme 2 bucks worth." When they say, "Do you want tall, grande , short, venti. . ." I'm gonna say, "You figure it out. Here's my 2 bucks. Give me as much coffee as that'll buy." And if they have to fill the thing up three-quarters of the way, or give me a cup and a half, that's their problem.

So next time you walk into a Starbucks…just walk up to the counter and say "Give me a buck fifty's worth of decaf," and see what they do. It's kind of like Alice's Restaurant. If we can get the whole country doing this, I think we may get them to stop this ridiculousness.

So whadda ya say? Are you with me on this? Good.

Wanna go out for a cup of coffee?

only the

mediocre can

always be at

their best.

—H. L. Mencken

The October Surprise: "Just Say No!"... to 3:00 P.M. Sunsets

(Ray)

Let's face it, Standard Time sucks rotten kiwi. Fall is a fabulous time of year. Except for the occasional frosty air that reminds us we're about to head into 8 months of weather from the Pleistocene, it's actually kind of nice outside. It's a chance to wear all that cute L.L. Bean flannel you got for Christmas last year and not feel like the inside of a brick oven. But do we get to enjoy it? No. Why? Because by the time we're all out of work, it's so stinkin' dark that you're lucky if you can get to your car without bonking yourself on a telephone pole.

Who's behind the great Standard Time conspiracy? We're not sure, but we think that, whenever it started, parents and large multinational companies had their grubby paws in it. Why? Simple. These are the two main forces in society that don't want us to have any fun at the end of the day. They want us to come home, do a little homework, have supper, watch prime-time sitcoms, forget about revolution, and hit the hay—so we'll be nice and fresh and ready to be exploited or indoctrinated all over again the next morning.

Enough of this horse hockey! In a Magliozzi administration (did I mention we're running in November?), we will order all clocks set forward a minimum of three hours every fall. (The exact number of hours will be left to personal preference. You decide what's right for you.) You'll go to work in the dark, and during your morning break for a cup of joe you can kick back and watch the sun rise. Then, when quitting time rolls around, you can get out and enjoy the day and still have three hours of bright, refreshing sunshine. Imagine: It's November 28, a sunny day in downtown Topeka. It's 7 P.M. and the kids are on their third game of kickball out in the street. You've just finished rebuilding the carburetor in your '63 Dart, and you still have plenty of time to walk the dog and cook up a feast on the gas grill in the backyard. This isn't some made-up Lewis Carroll tale. It's life under yours truly. And we can do it with a simple executive order.

In the meantime, here's an idea. How about we boycott Standard Time and keep Daylight Saving Time? When October 27, 28,—or whatever the appointed day—rolls around, forget about changing the clocks. Don't fall back an hour. Don't even think of changing that hour hand. The powers of oppression, who started this seasonal-affective-disorder-inducing nonsense to begin with, will be down on their knees and ready to talk turkey.

Our proprietary studies (done by Paul Murky, of Murky Research, Inc.) have shown that our country's reserves of daylight are perilously low. We must continue to save precious daylight. The "Spring ahead, Fall back" policy has proven itself to be complete B.S. We ask you, is darkness the kind of legacy we want to leave our children?

This policy will strike at the very hearts of all Americans. Our country has suffered through decades—if not centuries—of "standard" time. For six months of every year, millions of Americans have gone to work in the dark and come home in the dark. It's time for this senseless persecution to end.

HA HA HA

... And They Don't Even Break a Sweat!

(Ray)

Professional golfers, in my humble opinion, are a bunch of elitist crybabies (though I must admit they do dress well). A couple of years ago, their association, the PGA, cried foul when a fellow named Casey Martin tried to join the PGA tour. It seems that this fellow Martin had a circulation problem in his right leg that prevented him from walking the course like the other golfers, although there was nothing that prevented him from hitting the ball. He could do that perfectly OK. I guess you'd call what he had a handicap. So he asked if he could use a golf cart instead of walking the course. PGA members immediately began the crybaby routine. They said things like "If he wants to be a PGA golfer, then he has to be a *real man* and walk the course like the rest of us—not ride in some sissy golf cart."

Now, if ever there was a bunch of professional athletes not deserving of the title *real men*, it's PGA golfers. Don't get me wrong, I have great respect for their ability to hit the ball so accurately and so far. I've always been impressed that they can even find the ball after hitting it, something I could never do when I played. And I will admit that I love watching golf on television on a Saturday afternoon. I mean, nothing puts me to sleep like a golf match. The hushed tones, the idyllic setting, the glacial pace of the game. It all induces the kind of sleep that only a baby enjoys. It's just wonderful.

But I have to admit that I lost what little respect I had for the PGA and its members when they tried to ban Casey Martin. What a classless move! I guess they were afraid that some guy with a legitimate physical problem was going to outperform the able-bodied members and take all the prize money. What a bunch of undignified losers—in my humble opinion.

So I propose that the PGA should adopt some rule changes in an effort to redeem itself. First of all, they should allow anyone who makes the cut the right to play without having to go to court. If you can put the ball in the hole on a par with the other players, no pun intended, you get to play. Walking from hole to hole is hardly part of the game. Second, they should allow players to take tee shots while other players are still on the fairway. All that ducking and weaving and diving for cover would certainly add an exciting and desperately needed new dimension to the game and make it more of a sport. Third and most important, they ought to allow a little more fan participation. What's with all these hushed tones? I think golf fans ought to be allowed to jeer and heckle and yell out anything they want while someone's taking his shot. After all, every other sport allows it.

Let's look at hockey, for example. You've got players on ice skates who have to contend with opponents moving at 40 miles an hour who are trying to dismember or maybe even decapitate them when they're not looking. Then you've got the puck, 5 ounces of the hardest rubber known to humankind, flying around the rink at maybe 100 miles an hour, and maybe at your head. In addition, you've got the fans screaming out the most vile obscenities about your sainted mother and throwing things like beer cans and live squid on the ice while you're trying to play. Wow! These guys **are** real men.

Golfers, on the other hand, demand complete silence from their fans while taking aim in a serene environment at a ball that's not even moving. I think these snobs ought to be brought down a peg or two if they want the rest of us to think of them as athletes. I really do hope they see the light and adopt my recommendations. It would certainly make the game more exciting, and might even keep me awake on Saturday afternoons.

Lies, Damn Lies, and Magazine Surveys: A Surprising Result

(Tom)

There I was, reading some issue of *Money* magazine. Not that I *have* any money. I was reading it to find out how to *get* some money. And instead of money, the feature article is "The Best Places to Live." So, I give it a glance. I figure the best place to live in the USA must be, like, Honolulu. But the best place to live, according to the wackos at *Money* magazine is . . . Madison, Wisconsin!

Being a professional researcher, I ask myself, "How did they come to this, to say the least counterintuitive conclusion?" I mean, the last time I spoke to anyone in Madison, it was 25 below zero (not counting the wind chill), and to my knowledge, the city's greatest contribution to the rest of the world is some kind of orange cheese. Am I wrong on this?

And so, I read on to find out how they reached this conclusion. I mean, the "Best Place in the Country" is a rather bold claim, no? Well, it turns out that they did a survey of the residents of 300 cities and asked them to rate their *own* towns on the basis of a bunch of things like economy, health care, housing, etc. And Madison *still* wins.

Perception Is Reality

First, let's look at the methodology. *Money* magazine goes out and asks a bunch of people questions like "How good is health care in your city?" "How good are the educational facilities in your city?" "How good are the leisure time activities in your city?" They rate everything on a scale of 1 to 100. Now if all these people have never been anywhere else, how would they know "how good" any of this is? I mean, compared to what? Their only benchmark is the past. So, if there was never anything to do, but you just got cable TV, you'd say, "Wow! Does it get any better than *this*?"

Another benchmark they have, of course, is pain. And to their credit, the good people of Madison did rate "the weather" at 11 points out of 100. So, they're not completely out of touch. This is a place where the average *high* temperature in the winter is 20 degrees F. That's the *average high*. They didn't mention the low. But, clearly this is a place where you have to move briskly to keep your thighs from freezing together.

And look at some of the other ratings for this "Best Place to Live":

ahhhhh!

Crime 49
Housing 27
Leisure 8
Arts 28

When you include the weather rating of 11, 5 of the 9 factors are absolutely stinko! So, what's so good about Madison?

Well, the economy scored 94. That means everybody's working. Good. I guess the cheese industry had a bumper crop last year.

Health scored 99. I guess the hospitals have specialists in frostbite treatment.

And here's a biggie. "Transit," which I assume means public transportation, scored a whopping 85. But since leisure and arts scored so abysmally, this means that it's easy to get around—but there's no place to go.

But I suppose if *they*'re happy, what else matters? Perhaps perception *is* reality.

Here's how I look at it. What *Money* magazine did is fine. It's simply the title of the article that is *all* wrong. It shouldn't be "The Best Place to Live." It should be, "The Best Place to Live if You Already Happen to Live in Madison, Wisconsin, and Don't Know Any Better."

ahhhhh!

And My Brother Has the Ph.D. in Marketing?

(Ray)

My brother may have the Ph.D in marketing, but I, the younger, smarter brother, have come up with the greatest marketing idea of the century—in my humble opinion.

I was thinking about pool halls. When we were kids, we weren't allowed to go into pool halls because they were dark and dangerous places that awful people frequented and where nefarious things like gambling were done. Of course, as soon as we got the chance, we went right to the pool hall because it sounded exciting. We soon discovered that most pool halls were dark places full of lots of empty tables and a handful of strange-looking, maybe even nefarious-looking patrons. There was hardly anything exciting about any of them, but they did all have one thing in common regarding the pool tables. In every pool hall—nefarious or not—the tables were sacrosanct. Large scribbled signage admonished:

NO FOOD NEAR TABLES. NO SMOKING OVER THE TABLE! NO MOLECULES OF DIRT OR UNKNOWN SUBSTANCES ANYWHERE WITHIN 5 FEET OF THE TABLE.

Well, I guess about 20 years or so had passed since we last shot pool, when one night, we and our buddies Peppy and Vito decided it was high time we shot some 9 ball. Boy, were we in for a surprise! The pool halls we knew as kids were no longer extant. Gone were the dark expanses and drab interiors. Gone were the characters in the sharkskin suits and the pointy-toed shoes. These pool parlors of the '90s featured bright lights, live music, and attractive young waiters and waitresses serving beer and wine and *food*. There were pool tables, too, but absent from the mix was the feeling that the tables were somehow sacred.

Somewhere along the way, somebody figured out that they could make a hell of a lot of money if people could hang out around the pool tables and drink $4 beers and eat chicken wings. These new owners didn't care if you spilled a beer on the table or dropped a greasy chicken wing next to it. No problem. They'll just bring another table right in here for you. Would you like another round of drinks? This new breed of pool hall owner had figured out something. In contrast to the philosophy of his predecessors, he figured out that the tables didn't matter. They were just another place to rest your glass of beer, and if you happened to make a mess out of a table, so what? Well, it was a revelation to me, and I soon began to realize the parallel between the pool hall and—get this—public transportation!

Now, in Our Fair City we have a subway system, and when you enter the subway, you can't chew gum, you can't eat, you can't smoke. I don't think you can even talk. I guess it's probably the same in most cities. It's no fun. Not long ago, our esteemed producer Douglas Q. Berman was almost sent to prison for daring to bring a cup of coffee into the Metro in Washington, DC. In fact, they were ready to take him away in irons were it not for a deft move that allowed him to elude the arresting officer and slip into a subway car whose doors were just about to close and speed him off to the safety of the next station. The point here is very simple: Public transportation isn't fun. In fact, like the old pool halls, it's boring, it's dark, and it's depressing. Furthermore, there are hardly any volunteers, i.e., people using public transportation because they *want* to. I figure the majority of the people riding our subways or buses or commuter trains are doing so because they *have* to. They either don't have cars or can't afford to park near work, and sadly, the folks who run our public transportation systems know this and treat their passengers like cattle. If we want our public transportation systems to work, if we want people to ride public transportation so we can alleviate some of the traffic congestion in our cities, then we need to make it fun. Here's what I propose.

If we want to attract volunteers to our public transportation system, we need to abandon this belief that the cars and the stations are sacred cows, and we need to lure people from their cars by offering things that they can't get in the privacy of their automobiles. I think, for example, that there ought to be a car where cigar smoking is allowed, just one car. In fact, they could even sell cigars right in the station. And if that car stinks at the end of the night when the trains stop running, they can hose it down and even fumigate it.

By the same token, eating and drinking should be allowed in some of the cars. I think you should be able to get a cappuccino and a brioche in the morning, and if you spill the crumbs and the coffee all over the place, big deal. They'll clean it out. In fact, they'll have so much business, they won't even have to clean the cars if they don't want to. If they get too dirty, they can just throw them away and buy new ones. They'll have so much money from all the extra riders, they won't know what to do with it.

I'd like to see commuter train cars that offer aromatherapy—you know, some pleasant sylvan scent to help soothe away your troubles at the end of a long, hard day. For those who want a little more excitement, we could have motif cars. I can see a Caribbean car with musicians playing steel drums and happy, happy music to lift your spirits at the end of a difficult day, or maybe a string quartet for our classical music aficionados. I think belly dancers might go over pretty well, too. If fact, I know belly dancers would go over pretty well.

Anyway, you get the idea. We need to make public transportation fun. But we're so hung up on making sure that the subway stations stay clean and the cars stay clean that we've forgotten the real reason that we need public transportation: to get the greatest number of people out of their cars and off our crowded and gridlocked roads. Just think how great it would be if we could unclog our roads and reduce the air pollution in our cities by getting lots more people to ride our trains and buses. We have a choice. We can try to force people to ride public transportation, which is certainly one way to do it, but I prefer the approach of making it fun and something that everyone wants to do. Believe me, if you had belly dancers and things like fashion shows and cigar smoking and all that, people would be riding those trains to work like crazy. You wouldn't have to think about forcing anyone to do it. I know I would enjoy sitting in a car with a bunch of people smoking some nice Dominican cigars or maybe even getting a neck and shoulder massage during my ride home. That's what I want. I'd be there every day.

Now if this isn't the marketing idea of the century, I don't know what is. Even sliced bread pales by comparison.

And they gave the Ph.D. in marketing to my brother. Go figure.

The Hollywood Manifesto

(Tom)

I'm mad as hell and I'm not going to take it anymore!

Just what ARE we going to do about Hollywood? Does there exist, anywhere else in the world, a community so tacky, so ignorant, so irresponsible, so mercenary—and so rich? On our money.

A few months ago I went to see a flick titled *The Rock,* starring Sean Connery And this did it for me. I may never go to a movie again. For 15 or 20 minutes it was actually interesting. Sean Connery is always good. Then the Hollywood Schlocks took over. What had started out as a reasonably interesting story with some reasonably interesting characters suddenly degenerated to utter nonsense with a 20-minute car chase. From there, it further degenerated to blood, gore, killing, more blood, more shooting.

I realized later that what we had here was a 20-to-30-minute story which had been stretched to 2 hours. This, I guess, is the usual formula. I suppose it does keep a lot of special effects people and a lot of stunt persons off the streets, but gee . . .

So what?

There are a couple of things worth talking about. First, think about who we're making rich. Second, what effect does it have on the world?

Making Morons Rich

There is Sly. Now, if ever there was a man in need of a big brother, here he is. He has made several hundred million dollars carrying around that cannon and blowing up everything and everyone in sight. Granted, he couldn't get a job doing much of anything else. I'm happy that he's living comfortably. I suppose if he hadn't been kept busy doing what he does, he could have become a real criminal. But Sly—enough already!

Then there is Arnold. This Neanderthal mutant sometimes appears to actually have some semblance of a brain. Obviously he doesn't, or he wouldn't continue to do the things he does. Surely, he doesn't need the money.

Then, of course, there are all the people directing, producing, gaffing, best boying, and all the rest. Many of these are the ignorant, tacky, irresponsible mercenaries referred to above.

And we're making them all so rich that they can afford to buy small countries.

Is this good? Of course it's not good. Everyone—except those getting rich—admits that it's not good. Is it just a coincidence that crime and violence in the real world have escalated so dramatically in the past couple of decades during which these movies have been made?

Now, I'm not so naive as to believe that Hollywood schlock is the sole cause of all the social ills in this country. But is it contributing? Of course it is. Is it doing any good? Of course it's not. Anything that contributes should be stopped, unless it contains some other benefits.

Name one.

The Hollywood types say that their "art" is simply the mirror of society and reality. They say there is no causal link between what they do and what happens in the world. Bull! Everyone without a vested interest knows that they clearly are affecting attitudes and behaviors. When we see violence, we become desensitized to it.

Would you or I see one of these movies and consider blowing up a building? NO. But how about a teenager with raging hormones—the very segment that frequents these movies?

Hollywood answers that millions of kids see these movies and are good, honest, law-abiding citizens. No one asserts that the movies affect everyone. Do they have to affect everyone in order to be bad? How many wackos does it take to blow up a building and kill hundreds of innocent people? One or two people can wreak greatly disproportionate havoc. How many people does it take to murder your son or daughter? Isn't just one, one too many?

So, What to Do?

What can we do about this? I mean, why are we allowing these tacky morons to get so rich? Morons with no social responsibility. And are we helplessly in their grasp?

We are not helplessly in their grasp. Here's why.

THEY NEED OUR MONEY. They get our money from the movie theaters. So, what if we boycott ALL MOVIES shown in ANY movie theater that shows these ridiculously violent movies? We know that much of the movie revenue comes from teenagers. But not all of it. It doesn't do any good for us to boycott the specific movie; there will be plenty of teenagers to bring money to THAT movie. But we CAN boycott the entire movie theater.

There aren't many independently owned movie theaters around anymore, but there are some. Their owners might have a little social consciousness. So, next time you feel the urge to go to a movie, just avoid the theaters that are advertising Arnold and Sly and Bruce. And if all the theaters in your town are owned by some international conglomerate, stay home. Or visit a friend. Or read a book.

If you're mad as hell and want to do something about it, here's a suggested set of actions.

1. Boycott the theaters. Simply refuse to give them your money if they insist on showing Sly, Arnold, Bruce, and others of their ilk.
2. Insist that your kids boycott the theaters, too. The kids—who provide much of the movie revenue—probably get their money from you. I refuse to let my kid go to the blood-and-gore movies, but I stupidly

give him the money to see different movies in this same theater. No more!

3. Tell the theater what you're doing and why. Write a letter. Tell the manager of the theater what you're doing.

4. Tell everyone you know. (And tell the manager of the theater that you're telling everyone you know.)

5. Post the Manifesto shown on page 144. Put it in supermarkets, on bulletin boards at work—anywhere you can that will get others to tell these theaters that we're mad as hell.

6. Use the power of the internet to E-mail your friends.

7. Make up a Movie Fecal Roster of movies that shouldn't have been made. Movies that are doing society no good—and probably a lot of harm.

8. Let your friends know which movie theaters you're boycotting. Make up a Theater Fecal Roster as well.

I'm sure there are a few moviemakers left who know the difference between art and schlock. Let's get them back. And let the tacky morons find real jobs.

Here's the manifesto. Make a few thousand copies—or tear it out of this book.

DON'T CONTRIBUTE TO THE HOLLYWOOD VIOLENCE

*P*lease help stop the production of movies that contain killing and other forms of violence. Although Hollywood refuses to admit that such movies influence impressionable young people, it doesn't take a brain surgeon to figure out that these movies are certainly CONTRIBUTING to the mayhem in our society. They are certainly not helping the situation. Some people have decided that one way to get Hollywood's attention is to boycott not just the movies themselves—which you probably already do—but also the movie THEATERS that continue to show such movies. Refuse to give them your money. Money is the only language they understand. If you have the time, write a letter to the theater manager and explain that you are boycotting his or her theater—and explain why.

Thanks for helping.

The Power of 2: Wherein the Automotive Philosopher-King Discloses His Plan for World Peace

(Tom)

Isn't it interesting how we humans adapt? I mean, think about the kinds of things we put up with! So much of what we'll accept is a function of what we get used to—what we're conditioned to accept as acceptable. Not that it's always good. Remember the anecdote you heard in Psych. 101? If you put a frog into a bucket of boiling hot water, it'll jump right out. Put the frog into a bucket of luke-warm water, where it feels pretty good, and it will just sit. Then, if you gradually increase the temperature of the water in small increments until it's boiling, the frog will stay, until it literally gets cooked to death. The theory is that at no time is the temperature very much different from what it was a few minutes before, so the frog never notices. And then he's dead.

People are evidently as stupid as frogs in this respect. (George Carlin, in his stand-up comedy routine, says "You'd be amazed at how stupid the average person is. Even worse, half the people are even stupider than THAT.") We seem to be willing to accept outrageous conditions if the situation is never very much different from what it used to be.

Think about driving a car in an average city, in this presumably civilized country. Try to view what you see every day as you would view it if you had never seen it before; you would be outraged at the degree of incivility, aggression, and outright hostility that's exhibited by many drivers. (Or is it *most* drivers? I'd guess that most readers of the sentence would deny that THEY are included in the "many.") My research indicates that you probably aren't included. Those exhibiting the kind of really detestable driving behavior that exists on most roads are really a small percentage of the total. But just like terrorists, who make up an infinitesimal proportion of the population, they have a far greater affect on our lives than their small (absolute) numbers would suggest. Our government spared no expense or effort in tracking down the perpetrators of the World Trade Center and Oklahoma City bombings. Yet, hardly any serious effort is expended on controlling the situation on the roads.

I'd like to present the thesis that the driving problem is as grave as the bombings. After having (hopefully) convinced you of the severity of the problem, I'd like to then suggest solutions—some outrageous. Drastic conditions sometimes require drastic action.

Violence, Aggression, and Hostility

There's an interesting analogy between driving a car and the entertainment industry. Critics of the industry argue that the violence and mayhem so prevalent in movies and television have a profound effect on behavior, and thus encourage further violence in society. Since violent behavior is made so commonplace, they argue, we become desensitized to it: it becomes expected, normal, and therefore acceptable behavior in real life. (Let's call this the Causation Theory.)

On the other hand, the protectors of the rights of free expression (who frequently also happen to make handsome livings by portraying violence) contend that TV and cinema simply *reflect* reality (so let's call it the Reflection Theory). Furthermore, they continue, entertainment—to be entertaining—should be "larger than life" and must, of necessity, involve fantasy. Rambo, they argue, is simply a modern-day manifestation of the very same principles embodied in the works of Mother Goose or Shakespeare. The fantastic depictions of violence do not provoke violence. Humans are able to separate fantasy from reality. Proponents of this argument point to the millions of viewers who are exposed to the media violence and do not commit acts of violence. (Those familiar with statistics know that this is a specious analysis technique.) Even children know that a big bad wolf cannot really blow down a pig's house (so they say).

Driving a Car

Similar conflicting hypotheses exist in the context of driving. We can argue that driving a car does not, in itself, cause hostile and belligerent behavior; rather, it simply provides a context in which people express their basic inherent belligerence and feelings of hostility. We're just animals: Driving is simply a *reflection* of our basic nature. It is readily admitted that driving does indeed provide a context rife with opportunities for aggression. Behavioral scientists long ago identified our basic needs for power and control. And "getting ahead" takes on quite a literal translation on the road. The insulation, protection, and additional power of the vehicle add fuel to the fire, so to speak. Physically smaller women in Pontiac Firebirds, for example, suddenly become superior to much larger men in wimpy Honda Civics. The physically less powerful have an opportunity to exert a power far beyond their natural capabilities. The socially disadvantaged gain similar opportunity; money in the bank and a Ph.D. are no match for a giant SUV in this game.

So the aggression and hostility we see on the highways are inevitable. And not just inevitable, but even good. The vehicle is the great equalizer, providing the "social justice" of the jungle which civilization has destroyed. All those who feel that they have somehow been mistreated, subjugated, taken advantage of, etc. have the opportunity to get even in their cars.

So Who's Right?

Come on! Of course we all know who's right. (Unless you make your living in Hollywood. Even then, you know who's right. You just can't afford to admit it.)

Remember the frog? Remember Pavlov's dog? Yes, at some level, we *are* all animals, and as such we are subject to the same laws of conditioning. Any thinking person who does not have a vested interest must admit that the Reflection Theory is bullshit. Of course we're influenced by the aggression and violence we see around us. The American Psychological Association recently concluded that violence is a learned behavior. The frog part of us, after a while, accepts its conditions as not much different than they used to be. So we sit there. And pretty soon we're dead. It doesn't take a brain surgeon's brain to figure out that the obsession with violence in movies and television has had a profound effect on those who see it. Those who are conditioned to accept it as acceptable. Are we all influenced by it to the extent that it affects our behavior? Yes! All of us. It "teaches" all who view it that power and bravado are the ultimate winners. And even if you are mature enough and civilized enough to overcome the suggestion that you can solve problems by physical force—even to the extent of finding a gun and killing your opponent—some are not. And the ones who are not mature enough or intelligent enough are precisely the ones to whom the TV and Hollywood violence is targeted.

There can be no doubt that violence and aggression are learned behaviors. And just as they are learned from parents, role models, TV, and movies, so are they learned on the highways. Every day, the power and efficacy of hostile, aggressive behavior are reinforced. If violence works for Rambo in the jungle, it will work for the bully on the freeway. Why not? Every day we see the bully literally getting ahead. He cuts you off and he is ahead of you. And if it works on the freeway, then it should work in other contexts. If you're not pleased with your wife, beat her up. Your kids, the same. A kid from another gang? Shoot him.

So we can't allow this to go on. We simply can't allow the despicable behaviors to be reinforced every day. To take their toll on this country and the world as they have done. We have to take drastic measures to stop what's happening on the roads because now we see that it doesn't stop there! All hostile, aggressive behavior, no matter what the context, influences all parts of our lives. Either it reinforces our belief that it works, or it desensitizes us, no matter how outrageous the behavior in absolute terms. If watching Rambo has an effect, then so does watching a bully on the freeway.

The other day I witnessed a sad confrontation. A driver (older, white, male) started to take a right turn on red (legal, if no cars or pedestrians otherwise have the right-of-way). A pedestrian (young, black, female) was attempting to cross the intersection (she had the right-of-way). The white male driver almost hit her. Her reaction was explosive. She screamed, swore, and hollered obscenities. The driver, realizing his mistake, apologized, but to no avail. Clearly, for her there was more significance to the confrontation than was immediately apparent. Would she have reacted this way if her mother, for example, had been driving the car? I think not. The age, color, and gender of the driver clearly evoked a response greatly disproportionate to the circumstances. And even worse, whatever stereotypical personality characteristics she had previously ascribed to that man were reinforced by the confrontation. Bystanders could almost hear her thoughts: "White supremacist honky bastard thinks he owns the goddamn road and doesn't have to give the [deserved] right-of-way to *any* low-life black bitch!" It was awful.

I hope you're at least somewhat convinced that the problem deserves far more attention than it has received. So what to do?

A Problem Well Defined Is a Problem Half-Solved

When we're faced with problems of this sort, there's a tendency to look for an elegant and global solution—one simple change in law or policy that will solve the entire problem. But sometimes complex problems don't have simple solutions, because they have many causes rather than one. I don't think there is a single universal cause for the problems on the roads. And I think it's possible that by carefully identifying the sources of the problem, we might be able to find solutions to the individual pieces.

I've spent the past year driving around with a tape recorder, observing and recording instances of confrontations on the highways of Massachusetts. Beginning on page 152, I'll describe what I've observed and the conclusions I've drawn from these observations. I'll also suggest some solutions. I'll be brutally frank, because I think it's time to call a spade a spade and force the people who can do something about the problems to get off their butts and DO IT! I hope the discussion above has convinced YOU that the problem is serious, that it has far-reaching implications, and that we MUST do something about it.

So Who Can Do Something About It?

Many of the confrontations I've observed derive from the fact that drivers don't obey the rules of the road. Some of these "rules" are actually laws, and some are simply commonsense golden rules of civility and good manners. Let me address some of the reasons why this happens (there are several). Knowing how important it is to solve the problem(s), and that it IS time to do something about it, many of the solutions become obvious. I'm sure you've thought of many of them; they fall into the category of "Why don't they . . . " It's just that no one has thought the situation was important enough to actually institute any of the changes that are necessary. We've been sitting in the slowly warming water, and we're about to be dead.

So, why don't "people" obey the rules? Here's what I've concluded after a year of driving around with my tape recorder. People don't obey the rules because:

1. Some don't know the rules.
2. Some are animals and don't care about the laws (and don't care about much of anything, for that matter, except themselves).
3. Some do know the laws, and they are not animals, but they have been conditioned to disobey the laws.
4. Some feel they are forced to disobey the laws and to put aside the common rules of courtesy.

Let's think about WHO can, and should, do something about each of these.

1. Don't know the rules.

Why the hell don't they know the rules? The answer is simple. Because we give a driver's license to anyone! In Massachusetts, the written portion of the driving test has 20 multiple-choice questions! Twenty! Really! Out of the hundreds, if not thousands, of situations one encounters on the road, the Massachusetts Registry of Motor Vehicles thinks they are adequately represented by 20 questions? It's worse than that. One need answer only 14 of the 20 correctly to pass the test—i.e., a grade of 70% (a very low C-). So, if luck (good for him or her, bad for the rest of us) is with any idiot who takes the test, he's got a license if he can manage to maneuver a vehicle along city streets for about 5 minutes without banging into too many people or things. What the hell are we thinking? In most states it's more difficult to get a license to cut someone's hair!

So does it take a brain surgeon to figure out what needs to be done here, and who needs to do it? It's obvious, isn't it? First, the test should be hundreds of questions. The test should include not only questions of law, but questions involving the commonsense civility that we now allow each individual to construct and interpret for himself. Remember George Carlin! "You wouldn't believe how stupid the average person is. And worse than that, half the people are even stupider that THAT!" And we allow them to make up any damn rules they think make sense? Really, now! Let's not forget the perspective here. These people are both causing and acting out the hostility and aggressive behavior on the roads. The very same behavior that is being translated into our personal lives.

And what's this 70%? The ONLY passing grade should be 100%! Speaking of brain surgeons, would you want YOURS (should you need one) to have answered only 7 questions out of 10 to prove he or she was qualified? Would you put your life in his hands? Well, you put your life in the hands of millions of people who did just that! Every day.

And if you don't score 100%, you take the test again and again. You can't drive until you do.

And then, you take it again EVERY TIME you attempt to renew your license. (Do you honestly believe that YOU could pass the [simple] driver's license test in your state now?)

Some will argue that such a system would put such a burden on departments of motor vehicles (DMVs) that chaos would ensue. Sure it would. But what do we have now? I'd rather have the chaos in a few dozen buildings than on every road in the country. It has to be done, just as stronger drunk driving laws had to be passed and enforced. Let us not forget that much of the reason "we" allowed drunk driving to go relatively unpunished for so long was that the bureaucrats (the very people to whom we had entrusted the responsibility of enacting and enforcing laws against it) were either lazy or paralyzed with fear that they themselves would be subjected to those laws—politicians and judges! Repeat violators were given the token "slap on the wrist" because judges knew that they themselves had been guilty of driving while under the influence. "Oh, what the hell! The guy just had a few drinks. We all do that at one time or another. License suspended for 2 weeks." Not until MADD (Mothers Against Drunk Driving) forced politicians and judges to do what we had hired them to do, did the situation change.

So the first step is to force the bureaucrats to do the jobs for which we pay them.

2. The Animals

Some people really are just animals. They're crude, insensitive, and pretty much hopeless. They care only about themselves. They are sociopaths, and driving is simply one manifestation of their psychosis. They weave in and out of traffic and use the break-down lane to gain advantage of all in their path. They WILL be first!

Here's another anecdote that shows how aggressive driving behaviors cross over into other contexts. A few weeks ago, my family and I stopped at a Dunkin Donuts coffee shop. A woman in a small car sped through the parking lot and parked in the clearly marked handicapped spot. She walked into the shop behind us. There was a short line at the counter. This woman edged herself to the front of the line, ahead of 5 or 6 people who had clearly arrived before she did. I lost it (to the great embarrassment of my kids, I might add). I asked her why she thought her need for coffee was somehow more important than the needs of the 6 people in front of her. And by the way, by what right did she take the handicapped parking place? She moved back in the line, but never answered the second question. Nor was she embarrassed. Her behavior was perfectly acceptable—to her.

There are two aspects to the situation regarding animals. One is that the animals are allowed on the roads despite their despicable behavior, and the second is that the vehicles they drive provoke and encourage their behavior.

First, the people. We know why they exhibit the selfish, inconsiderate behavior. Because they are selfish, inconsiderate people. The real question is why the rest of us have allowed them to persist in their behavior. One answer is that the police don't do their jobs. (We'll talk more about the police later.) But even if the police do their jobs, they simply can't be everywhere. Most of the time that an animal cuts into a line of cars, or tailgates with his/her high beams on, the police aren't there. But YOU ARE! I AM! But there doesn't seem to be anything we can do about it. Really? After all, there are far more of us than there are of them. We're just not organized. So they get away with it, which reinforces their belief that they CAN get away with it, and they persist.

This one really requires some creativity and maybe drastic measures. But let's remember the importance of the problem; their aggressive behavior is teaching the immature and less intelligent among us that aggression is not only acceptable, it WORKS. So every day we nurture a new generation of aggressive and hostile people. People who extrapolate the aggression on the roads to their daily lives and beat their wives and kids; or shoot people who "get in their way." (The implication of these words is not an accident, but shows the mechanism by which the behavior gets translated from highway to everyday life.) So here's an idea.

We Ain't Gonna Take It Anymore

What if during one hour a week—say Monday, from 9 A.M. to 10 A.M.—we organized? For that one hour, we, ALL OF US, will not allow it to happen. After all, when the animal cuts into a line of traffic, SOMEONE lets him in. No more. You stop. We all stop. Traffic gets backed up for miles. We use the magic of modern technology—cellular phones—to call the police. We wait until they arrive (I know this is coffee time for many police, but this is serious). For that one hour every week, we will not allow the madness to continue. Every bully will be forced to stop and be humiliated; to see the force of the thousands of us against the one of him. We all learned about bullies on the school playground many years ago. Give him an inch and he takes a mile. But let him know immediately that you aren't going to take it and he backs off. Well, the collective "we" aren't going to take it. A drastic, perhaps, but simple use of classic operant conditioning. It won't take too many days for the animals to get the message (and the summonses!). And the punishment must be harsh (like suspension of the license for a week or two, followed by REAL enforcement of the suspension. For example, by assigning a policeman to actually watch this bum's house for a few days. And if he drives during the suspension period, his license is suspended for a year! Sure the police will be busy. But how much coffee can they drink?).

There's no doubt that Mondays will be chaotic. But at

least now it's constructive chaos. Our objective is to break the habits of those who have come to believe that we are too weak to prevent their despicable behavior. We are not.

You may have now reached the conclusion that I'm nuts. Maybe. But I'm not so nuts that I don't appreciate the difficulty of this scheme. I recognize how much courage it will take. First, courage on the part of municipalities to endorse the scheme. This includes not only the government and the police, but all the employers who must cope with everybody being late to work on Monday. Second, it takes courage on the part of individuals to take part in the exercise. We're all reluctant to be first. But someone will have the courage. And have you ever noticed how quick the rest of us are to come to the aid of the person with courage enough to show the way? You'll do it because you know it's the right thing to do; because you, too, have courage; and because you want to get back at those bastards who've been cutting you off all these years. Think about how great it will feel. Remember all those times you wished someone or something would stop the animals. It's sweet. It's really sweet.

Sounds good so far, doesn't it? There's one problem, though. If the animals know that Monday at 9 A.M. is a time to be civilized, they'll soon adapt. So, we have to trick them. Fortunately, it's easy to trick them because they're pretty dumb. For example, we know that they're not reading this book, because they can't read. The few who can, don't. So we're ahead of them already. But they might figure it out, so we have to keep changing the day and time—without their knowing it! So how do we inform the general public without informing the animals? Simple. We announce it on PUBLIC radio and PUBLIC television! So, while they are watching the wrestling (or is it rasslin'?) matches, we are plotting against them. Oh, it is SO good!

3. Conditioned to Disobey the Laws

If you take a high school course in "civics," you'll be told that legislators make the laws and the police enforce them. This isn't quite true. In many cases, the police make the laws as well. Consider this. The speed limit on most of the highways of Massachusetts, where I live, is 55 miles per hour, according to the posted signs. But neither the signs nor the legislature determines the speed limit. The real speed limit is 64 miles per hour. Because that's the speed which you must exceed to get stopped by most police in Massachusetts. The police have decided that 64 mph is OK, the law notwithstanding. By what right? Most drivers in Massachusetts (and probably the state in which you live) have become conditioned to driving 9 mph faster than the posted limit.

So when we bemoan the fact that the police can't be everywhere, it's irrelevant. (Actually, they are somewhere. In Massachusetts, we use the State Police as observers of construction projects. Any road construction, no matter how minor, must be "supervised" by the State Police. A local wit recently asked whether someone thought that the holes being dug were in jeopardy of being stolen!)

What's the real problem with all of this? It's the message that is being sent to the immature and less intelligent drivers. The message that breaking the law is OK if you don't get caught. We become conditioned to believe that the true limit is 64 mph and not 55. So now what happens to the poor guy who decides to obey the law? Have you ever tried to drive at 55 when everyone else is doing 65? 75? Some may argue that 65 really is OK. Maybe they're right. But what about doing 35 in a 25 mph zone? Is that OK, too? Sure. What about 35 in a school zone, where the limit is 20 mph? Why not? We have been conditioned to believe that the number on the sign bears no relation to the real speed limit. The police have taught us this.

I live on a residential street where the posted limit is 25. I frequently call the police to complain of speeders. They come for half an hour. I've watched them. In a half hour I usually can count 10 or 15 cars which are exceeding the limit. The police generally stop 1 or 2. I've stood there and looked at the radar. Car after car goes by doing 28 or 29 mph. The police let them go. "What the hell. It's only a few miles over the limit. I've done that myself." Sounds a lot like "So the guy had a few drinks. I've done that myself. So what?" The "so what" is that they are setting a precedent. The LAW says the limit is 25. Not 28! The conditioned response the police should be attempting to reinforce is that you had better be driving below the speed limit, not just a little above it. The speed limit is what it is because smarter, more concerned people have decided that on a residential street with lots of kids, 25 is the ABSOLUTE safe limit. It's not an average speed at which cars should be traveling. It's the LIMIT. The LIMIT for every single car.

It has even become unacceptable to obey the law if it causes difficulties for those who choose to disregard it. The speeder expects you to get out of his way. If you don't, you are subjected to high beams in your eyes, obscene gestures, and the like.

We don't expect the police to be everywhere. But here's what we can expect: We have the right to expect the police to condition the lawbreakers to punishment. So that when the police aren't there, the lawbreakers will think more than twice about breaking the laws. If you never get caught and you never get punished, then what's the incentive for following the rules? There is none. The government and the police allow US (stupid as they know we are) to decide whether a speed limit (or any other law) needs to be adhered to. They allow us to decide whether on this particular street we REALLY need to limit our speed to 25 mph. "They can't be too serious about this speed limit. I've exceeded it in front of the police and they never stopped me." The kid running out of a driveway chasing a ball will think it's serious.

I have stopped police in their cars to ask why they didn't stop a car that just went through a stop sign or a yellow light. The police don't take it kindly. But I won't stop doing it. And I'm asking you to do it, too. The 1 speeder that they stop or don't stop is not the issue. It's the precedent that they are setting; the message they are sending. Their job is to teach all of us that the sign is there for a reason. And that when it says speed limit, it means LIMIT!

4. Think They Are Forced to Disobey the Laws

This includes most of us. In a recent *USA Today* article, otherwise OK people said they believe that in order to survive in a world of animals, they must adopt the driving habits of the animals or be eaten by them—or, at best, taken advantage of. They don't participate in the illegal aspects of driving like the animals, but their behavior is nonetheless aggressive. "If I don't get there first, he'll get there first." "If I slow down, he'll get ahead of me." It does seem like the only way to survive, doesn't it? Maybe it is. But think about the cost of this "survival." We have become desensitized to the point that we've convinced ourselves it is necessary to drive in a stupid, uncivilized way. And therefore it's acceptable behavior. Except for the fact that we've thought it through, we're not much smarter than the frog. And worse than that, we've exacerbated the problem by our "defensive" behavior. And for every day that it goes on, we help to perpetuate the problem.

If You're Not Part of the Solution, Then You're Part of the Problem!

The vast majority of us have been prisoners of the status quo. We accept "what is" just as the frog does. Unless we take some positive steps, nothing good will happen.

> **What we haven't realized is the tremendous power we have.**

Think about this. If I give you 2 dollars today and double it every day, do you know how many dollars you'll get on the 27th day? 134 million! That happens to be about how many drivers there are in this country. So, what if I start with 2 drivers instead of 2 dollars? If I start with 2 drivers—say you and me—and we change OUR behavior toward 2 drivers today, and each of them changes his or her behavior toward 2 more tomorrow, then in 27 days, every driver will be affected. Powerful, isn't it? And how about this? What if the thing you and I do today is be extra nice to 2 drivers. And tomorrow, those 4 are extra nice to 8 more. Then 16, 32, 64, . . . 134 million! Think about this. If so much of what we do is influenced by what others do, what will happen if what we do is nice instead of aggressive and hostile? What if every time you come to an intersection, the other driver gives you the right-of-way? Every time you try to pull into a line of traffic, everyone stops to let you in? What if every time someone makes a mistake, he says "I'm sorry"? What will driving be like in 27 days? 54 days? 108 days?

Interestingly, it will probably be like walking! Think about it. If you bump into someone on the sidewalk, what do you do? You probably say "Sorry." You don't lash out. You don't make obscene gestures. You probably never think about who had the right-of-way! Think about it. Most times that pedestrians bump into each other, they both say "I'm sorry." (Interestingly, even the animals do this!)

The power of 2 has the power to change what is acceptable. Being nice could become the norm in 27 days! But it's even better than this. What if more than 2 of us start the ball rolling? For example if 50,000 people read this rant and implement the new strategy, all drivers will be affected in 11 days! Wow! So even if 1 pleasant confrontation isn't enough to change attitudes, in 27 days we'll all have had 3 pleasant ones. By this time next year the entire country will have changed its attitude. Every drive will be a pleasurable experience, like sharing the road with 134 million friends.

It gets even better. Remember the horrible story about the black girl and the honky—oops—white guy? Well, think about this. What if, as a few of us get this ball rolling, we make it a point to be extra nice not to people at random, but to people we think don't like us? If you're white, be extra nice to all other races. If you're old, be nice to teenagers. If you're a teenager, be extra nice to old folks. Men to women. Women to men. After all, if the attitudes against stereotypes are now being reinforced negatively, this idea will reinforce them positively. Can't you see it? The old geezer in the Chrysler New Yorker saying to himself, "Gee, these young kids aren't ALL bad, are they?" Same for Asians, whites, blacks, women, men.

This might really be a plan for world peace.

Percival Bananas:
The Zoo Rant

(Tom)

Picture this. You suddenly find yourself on the Planet of the Apes. Aside from the fact that you have to associate with Charlton Heston, life is not all that bad. Sure, you have to forage for food and live in a cave. And you can't access Cartalk.com or watch *Law and Order*. But the apes pretty much leave you alone—although a few do think it's fun to shoot at you with guns.

Then Percival Bananas—one of those tree-hugging apes with more money than brains—gets the following brilliant idea. "How about we capture a few of the 'people' and put them in cages so the kiddies can see what they look like? We'll treat them pretty well. You know, try to build a 'natural habitat' for them. Feed them every day. Even put a few males together with females and see what happens."

They get YOU.

Are you royally ticked off or what? Is it fun sitting there in the cage day after day? Is it fun having all those snotty-nosed little ape brats passing by the cage day after day—tossing peanuts (and rocks and Twinkie wrappers) at you? Do you miss your friends? Your family? Are the days endless? Does life suck or what?

OK. You can wake up now and come back to the Planet of the People. You know—the more intelligent, more sensitive, more compassionate species.

Why do we have zoos? You can try to rationalize this idea seven ways from Tuesday, but zoos are an incredibly cruel and abusive way to treat animals. And for what? So we can see what a panda looks like? You want to see a panda, go to China. You don't want to see a panda enough to go to China? Fine. Don't go. You won't miss the panda and the panda won't miss you. Proponents may argue that the animals are "better off" in the zoo than in their natural habitats. Percival Bananas probably said that, too. How did YOU like it? Did he ask you? Others may argue that they're saving certain species from extinction. Did the species ask them to do that? Oh, I forgot. We're so much smarter than they are that we know what's best for them. Percival Bananas thought that, too.

Whose idea was this, anyway? I'll tell you whose idea it was: rich people. It's true. Zoos date back to the ruling classes of China (according to my encyclopedia), who thought it would be "entertaining" to keep the animals.

Who the hell do we think we are? Leave the animals alone.

Every time you take your kids to the zoo, you're helping to support this cruelty. Plus, you're taking the chance that certain primates are going to fling their feces at you through the bars. And you know what? I don't blame them. Don't support the zoo. It ain't nice.

That's my opinion.

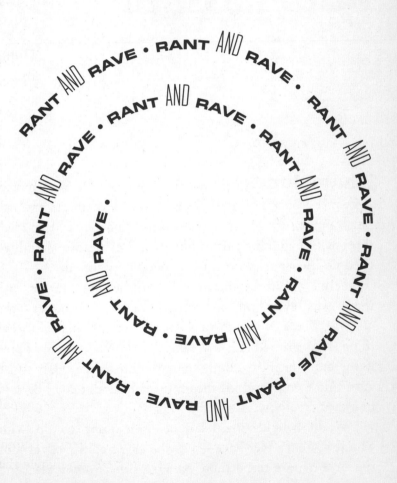

Monica What's-Her-Face and "Responsible" Journalism

(Tom)

I have long suspected that "responsible" journalists were just a bunch of schlocks with very few smarts and not much in the way of good taste (seems you can seldom trust those with highfalutin titles like the Fourth Estate). And we need no longer suspect, for now we know for sure.

There I was in the checkout line at the supermarket, and there was everybody's favorite trashy newspaper—the *Weekly World News*. Now, nobody actually believes anything that's printed in the *Weekly World News* (in my opinion), but, you must admit that it's fun to see what those guys find to report on. I mean, it really does take a certain brand of creativity.

Lo and behold, the headline—something to do with Monica What's-Her-Face—was the same as the cover stories in the more respectable papers: *Time, Newsweek,* and that last bastion of what's fit to print—the *New York Times*! Well, guys, you've finally shown yourselves for exactly what you are—and the word "responsible" does not leap to mind. Same goes for radio and TV newsrooms everywhere. You're all nothing but a bunch of jerks looking to fill another half hour with anything you can get your hands on—as long as you can keep those Nielsen ratings up to help pay your ridiculously exorbitant salaries.

Get this for rationalization! As I was channel surfing one night, I ran across one of those pseudo news programs where "responsible" journalists sit around and discuss what they're doing. I tuned in too late to know who any of these schlocks were, but one of them was from *Time* or *Newsweek*, I forget which. Here's how he justified his magazine's coverage of this Monica story: "This is what people are talking about, so it's our responsibility to write about it," he says.

You jerk! Don't you have it bass ackwards? Aren't people talking about it because you're writing about it? How would we even know about it if YOU hadn't decided that it was news? It's not news, stupid. And just because you've got a bigger vocabulary than I, it obviously doesn't qualify you to decide what's "fit to print."

I now have before me the latest issues of *Time*, *Newsweek*, and the *New York Times*. I'm canceling my subscriptions to them all.

My cancellation won't mean much. It won't mean anything to the network news shows if I don't watch. It will matter, however, if you happen to be a Nielsen family. If you are, I strongly urge you to avoid them all like the plague. But I do have to thank them all for proving quite conclusively what I have long suspected.

Another Microsoft Conspiracy

(Tom)

There exists in American culture today a polarization of values far more serious than political preference, race, or religion. It's a cultural difference, which one day could destroy the very fiber of the values on which this great country is founded. It's an issue that brings out feelings and emotions profound enough to cause a crack in the cosmic egg of life as we know it.

My friends, I refer, of course, to the Macintosh vs. PC controversy.

The very mention of this issue evokes a tirade of response that makes Bosnia-Herzegovina look like an afternoon tea. Aside from the gamut of emotion which the topic evokes, I think I have discovered a plot of such enormity, a plot so diabolical, that it boggles the mind.

And the discovery of this plot answers the question millions of computer users are asking: "Why are PCs winning the war?" Although it is true that there are many misguided souls (including everyone except me at *Car Talk*) who fanatically believe that Macintosh computers are easier to use, more intuitive, etc., etc., the truth is that there's little difference between them. Go ahead and start ranting, all you wacko right-brained fanatics. But the truth is the truth!

The real question is this: Given the small differences between Macintosh and PCs, why do 90 percent of computer users have PCs?

I'll tell you why. Because we've all become addicts! Tens of millions of unsuspecting computer users were given— free of charge—an innocuous little game when we bought or otherwise acquired Windows. You turn on your PC, and there it is. *Solitaire!* You try it. It's fun, so you try it again. Pretty soon, you forget to eat lunch. Then you forget to get a haircut. Then you forget to go home. When you finally do remember to go home, you can't, because you missed the train (and your pants are all wet).

The big question is, why does solitaire addiction affect PC users in far greater percentages than Macintosh users? Is it because Macintosh users are so much smarter and more sophisticated?

Hardly!

To answer that question, we must look at the mechanism that facilitates the addiction. Is it genetic? Is it a disease? Or is it simple conditioning? Several research studies suggest a nongenetic cause—pointing to subtle conditioning influences, much like those involved in smoking. But in this case, the culprit is not the tobacco industry. It is a far more insidious and unsuspected villain.

I don't play solitaire with real playing cards. I don't play it on my wife's dreaded Mac. Why on Microsoft? Because on Microsoft Solitaire I *win*! It has become clear to me that the odds of winning this game are far better than they ought to be. Have any of you noticed that the odds of winning virtual solitaire are *not* the same as real-world solitaire?

The game is fixed! It's rigged!

And *who* is responsible for this plot, this cabal, this conspiracy? Microsoft, that's who! Now why would Bill Gates, that little devil, have taken this simple little game and fixed it so we win? Bill ain't no dummy. He doesn't do anything without giving it a lot of thought. And, as we all know, he likes money. So the only reasonable conclusion is that Bill is getting us hooked; and should we *ever* consider a switch to the Macintosh camp, *whammo!* He shuts us off. We start losing. We get depressed. We need our fix, so we seek out a Windows machine and we're OK for another day.

Bill Gates is a drug dealer! Plain and simple.

Now repeat after me: "My name is Tom Magliozzi, and I'm a solitaire addict. *Help me! Help me!*"

The Deregulation of Airline Deregulation

(Ray)

Just what the hell have we accomplished by airline deregulation?

The Benefits

1. Competition has driven prices down. Now, every average Joe can go anywhere he wants to go.
2. He can go almost as often as he wants to.

That's it for the benefits. At what cost have we achieved these benefits?

The Costs

1. Vastly increased traffic in the air; there are hundreds more flights per day than there were before deregulation. This has led to:

   a. Horrendous automobile traffic at and around our airports.
   b. Delays at check-in, requiring passengers to arrive hours before departure.
   c. Terribly crowded and uncomfortable planes— due to reconfiguration of airplane interiors to maximize capacity. At 10 cents/mile/passenger, they just have to crowd us in like sardines.

2. Safety has been compromised—despite what the airlines would have us believe. Think about these things:

   a. All airlines have been unable to obtain enough truly qualified pilots and crews.
   b. How can maintenance be as diligent as it was before deregulation? The planes don't even stay on the ground long enough for the engines to cool off.
   c. Landings and takeoffs are more dangerous simply by virtue of their sheer numbers. In addition, landings and takeoffs occur when they shouldn't. Too many people are involved to delay or cancel a takeoff. Too many people— and therefore too many dollars—are involved in rerouting to safer airports in foul weather.

We have been fooled into believing that the Federal Aviation Administration has been our "watchdog." But it has not. First, we must remember that the FAA has a two-pronged mission:

1. To promote airline travel
2. To oversee and enforce safety.

These two aspects of the mission are enemies. To promote air travel AND at the same time regulate safety requires the wisdom of Solomon and the ethics of Jesus Christ—and the bureaucrats have neither. Our safety is in the hands of bureaucrats and businessmen; the incompetence of the former and the greed and sleaziness of the latter are legend.

It is time to end deregulation. Travel has been always a luxury of the upper class, and so it should be. If airfares doubled tomorrow, a large percentage of flights would be canceled. Mr. Average Joe would stay home. We would travel less—and enjoy it more. The airlines would have the time to maintain the planes. A greater percentage of pilots would be competent. Marginal weather conditions would prompt cancellations and delays. And some of us would live longer.

If God had wanted me to run, he'd have had someone chasing me • If God had wanted me to run, he'd have had someone chasing me • If God had wanted me to run, he'd have had someone chasing me.

Walking

(Ray)

Do we really need *Walking* magazine?

What's wrong with us? Do we need advice for everything? Can't we do anything on our own? I, for one, don't need too much advice on walking. About one page could do it.

Now I think I learned the basics at about 13 months, and by the time I was four, I was a pro. And I don't think I need a regularly published magazine to provide continuing education. It's pretty axiomatic that if you want to get in shape, walking is a great way to do it. And I think the farther and the faster you walk, and the more hills you climb, the better shape you'll be in. Oh, yeah. Good walking shoes or sneakers might be a good idea, too. So that's about it. Please send me $34.50 for your subscription, and this month I'll send you a letter reminding you to get off your butt and walk to the store. Next month I'll encourage you to walk to work or maybe even the dry cleaners or the library. And in the coming months I'll provide you with even more exciting destinations, like walking to a lake. Perhaps I'll even reveal some secrets—like leaning forward when you're climbing steep hills. All for just $34.50 . . . We'll also send you some steak knives.

Water, Water Everywhere

(Ray)

I'm simply amazed at the number of people drinking bottled water these days, to the tune of about a dollar a gallon or, in the case of the European stuff, more like a dollar a quart. It's ridiculous. What is bottled water anyway? Well, it's water that's been put into bottles. Duh. In some cases, it's nothing more than water that's been subjected to some kind of simple filtration process, or it's simply water that's bubbling up from a spring or pouring out of a cleft in some mountainside, and they put it in fancy bottles and voila, they call it Czechoslovakian springwater. But for the most part, they're not doing much to it except putting it into the bottles and taking it to the stores. There's no refining; there's no reconstituting; no nothing. There's really not much filtering; in some cases, there's no filtering. There's nothing added, there's nothing subtracted, and they're proud of this. "Our water is pure springwater," the ads say. We do nothing to it. Then we charge you a dollar a gallon for it. Well, I guess it would be OK if they actually did something to it—you know, like desalination or fortification with vitamins and minerals, the way they do with milk.

Speaking of milk, producing milk is a real pain in the butt. First of all, you've got the cows, and of course you've got three or four different kinds of cows. Most people don't know it, but there are regular cows that make regular—you know—whole milk. And of course you've got your 1% cows and your 2% cows and the skim milk cows and the chocolate milk cows. (I don't really know how they do the strawberry and the coffee milk.) And then of course you've got to feed the cows, and you've got to do something with the tons of manure that they generate, and of course you've got to house the cows. You've got to take care of them when they're sick. You've got to help birth the baby cows. And of course the farmer has to get up at 5 o'clock in the morning to collect the milk. He's got to put it in containers, and of course he has strict health codes and restrictions to abide by. Then, once the farmer's done with it, someone else has to pasteurize it and then homogenize it. And naturally you have to refrigerate the stuff and then return to it all the vitamins that you destroyed when you pasteurized it. And finally, you've got to package and ship the stuff and sell it before it spoils. Geez! And with all that effort, milk is still cheaper than water.

And how about gasoline? There are huge costs involved in bringing gasoline to the pump. First of all, you have to find the crude oil, and that ain't easy. And it seems to be getting harder every year—at least that's what they tell us. It used to be just bubbling out of the ground where guys like Jed Clampett could find it, but now they have to drill down thousands of feet into the earth's crust through rock to find the stuff. And since they've used up all the stuff that was easily found, they now have to do this out in the ocean. And, of course, the oil companies have to build these drilling platforms that can withstand tsunamis. Then, once they've managed to get the oil out of the ground, they have to ship it to a refinery thousands of miles away. In addition, the stuff is difficult and dangerous to handle from both an environmental and a safety standpoint. And yet, with all these considerations, when you take out the federal and the local taxes, the stuff costs a hell of a lot *less* than bottled water. Hard to believe.

Well, I just don't know how we all got fooled into thinking we had to drink bottled water, but we have. I know I was perfectly happy drinking tap water. It's always tasted good to me, and it didn't seem to pose any threat to my health (although I did grow two extra fingers last year). And then, a few years ago, little stories started coming out in the newspaper and on the 11 o'clock news, about how the water in one community was tainted or they found this or that deadly chemical or certain harmful bacteria in the water, and all of a sudden, everyone wants to drink bottled water. You know, they couldn't give the stuff away 20 years ago and almost no one drank it. Back then, if you had awful-tasting water, I guess *you* got a filtration system for your home, or maybe you were one of the ones who drank bottled water. But for the most part, the vast majority of us were perfectly content drinking the stuff that came out of the tap. And we still should be.

I, for one, think there's a conspiracy at work here among the bottled water companies, the tailors, the chiropractors, and the American Medical Association. Like I said, I was happy drinking tap water, but my wife convinced me that we should have bottled water in our house. So we buy this contraption which consists of a clay jug on a stand and these 6-gallon—yes, 6-gallon—bottles of water. I can't tell you how many pairs of pants I've split open and how many times I've thrown my back out trying to put these bottles onto this contraption without spilling the stuff all over the kitchen floor.

So I think these guys are all in this together, and they're out to take our money. The guys at the tailor shop are making a fortune repairing my pants. It seems I'm at the chiropractor every 2 weeks, getting my back adjusted. "What did you do this time?" he asks. "I was putting a bottle on the stand and I threw my back out." He smirks, and I know he's saying to himself "It's working." And I know it's only a matter of time before I need a hernia operation. In case you didn't know it, these 6-gallon jugs of water weigh 50 pounds each.

What are we, nuts? We must be, because practically each and every one of us can go to our kitchen sink and turn the handle, and wonderful water comes out of the faucet for a fraction of a cent a gallon. And we're buying bottled water and risking life and limb lifting those bottles? Now it's my feeling that unless you've got tadpoles coming out when you open the faucet, you ought to just drink the stuff that your city is supplying to you because it's good enough. Sure, there are some bacteria in it, but you know what? That's OK, too. We just can't insulate ourselves from everything

that might be dangerous or harmful to us. If we drink puri-
fied water that has nothing in it except hydrogen and oxy-
gen, we're doing our immune systems a disservice. We are
denying our immune systems the opportunity to practice on
something relatively harmless, and they need that practice.
We need these bacteria in our water so that our immune systems can say, "Uh-oh, there's a bad guy. I'm going to go and
kill it." And if you don't let your immune system practice
on something, you'll find that it won't be there for you
when you really need it. You'll be done for. And the fact of
the matter is, if you drink this bottled water all the time and
then you mistakenly drink municipal water out of the tap,
it's going to be just like you went to Guatemala and drank
out of a sewer. You're going to be on the toilet for 2 weeks
because your body will have gotten unaccustomed to drinking the stuff that you should have been drinking all along.
That's my position, and I'm sticking with it.

Jock Itch?

(Tom)

OK. Here's something that will surely alienate all the "real guys." But who cares?

What the heck is this maniacal obsession with sports? Give us a break, will ya? I click through the 400 cable TV channels and 350 of them have either some idiotic game being telecast or someone *talking about* the game that has been—or is about to be—telecast. Man the only thing worse than actually watching TV sports is having to HEAR the Neanderthals TALKING about sports. Usually it's some jock talking about his "strategy."

Like we care what he thinks (which is usually something quite profound, like "Well, uh, I think we're gonna hafta win more games if we're gonna get into the play-offs")! Really? Now why didn't WE figure that out? I guess we're just not as intimately familiar with the nuances of the game as Neanderthal Ned. Oops, I forgot. It's spelled Gnedd, isn't it?

To make it even worse, the seasons for each sport go on forever. Baseball starts when it's snowing in most of the country and ends . . . when it's snowing in most of the country. Hockey goes into . . . like July.

A Proposal

Here's my proposal. Part of the reason that sports take up so much of our valuable TV space (which could otherwise be running *Baywatch* reruns) is that most of the games go on far too long. What for? Just to see who wins? Well, if that's all we're trying to do, we can tell who wins much sooner. For example, take basketball. These guys play for hours. BUT I've noticed something interesting. There appears to be a very strong correlation between who's ahead at the end of the first quarter and who wins. So, we could determine who wins by playing ONE quarter. (Do they call them quarters? Or periods? Or what? Did I mention I don't follow sports?)

Here's how it would work. Let's say the Buffalo Bull Droppings are playing the New York Carjackers. They play for ONE of those periods/quarters/things. The Buffalo Bull Droppings are ahead. By using the correlation coefficient (which I estimate to be about 0.8—but we could actually calculate it based on the last 500 years of games; well, it seems like 500 years to me). So, if it's 0.8, there's an 80% chance that the Carjackers will lose. So we set up a brief game of chance to reflect the odds (like a 5-sided coin with

4 heads and 1 tail). We flip the thing and proclaim the winner. Now all these 10-foot freaks can go elsewhere and do something more useful (like posing in $200 sneakers—or, maybe, feeding giraffes).

I realize it would be harder to find something useful for hockey players to do.

Here's another thought. Maybe we could turn this useless pastime into a far more meaningful activity. I mean, what the heck, if they HAVE to play, why not play for something besides money? Like why not use the silly games to settle international disputes—instead of killing people? Think of the possibilities—"Big Game Tonight at Eight! Serbs vs. Herzagovinians. Winner gets the country formerly known as Prince!"

Going to the Dogs: Pit Bulls, Rottweilers, and Testosterone Poisoning

(Ray)

Right at this very moment, I'm on the hairy edge of going 100% completely ballistic. But, before I do, I'm going to take a deep breath, slap on some Preparation R&R, and start this Rant and Rave out on the right foot (or paw, in this particular case) with an example of what I consider to be responsible dog ownership.

Ralph, Bruno, and Rambo

I have a buddy, Ralph, who owns a gas station in my neighborhood. Ralph has two Rottweilers that are positively humongous. We'll call these beasts Bruno and Rambo. Every few weeks, I drop by to say hello to Ralph and buy some gas. Each time I go in, Bruno and Rambo are lying there, chained to a block of steel that is permanently embedded in the concrete floor. The chains that go between the dogs and the anchor are not unlike the ones that Cunard uses to keep the *QE II* from drifting around Portsmouth harbor. The point is, these dogs are securely tied down.

Bruno and Rambo never make a peep when I approach them. They never wag their little nubs of tails, and they're never happy to see me. Bruno and Rambo have the canine version of the Timothy McVeigh blank stare. Ralph always says, "Don't worry! They'll never hurt you. They're gentle as can be." I, of course, can't help but think that they must be communicating telepathically: "Yeah, that right butt cheek—now that looks like a good snack!"

Bruno and Rambo are, for all intents and purposes, deadly weapons. Ralph knows that these dogs are dangerous. At the end of the day, when he closes the shop, he lets them have the run of the place—knowing that anyone who breaks in will be quickly inhaled. And, quite frankly, Bruno and Rambo would be well within their rights to take you out in that situation. I can accept that, under those circumstances.

Spike Comes Home

Here's what I can't abide: I can't abide the next-door neighbor who's stupid enough to think that having a Bruno or a Rambo as an unrestrained pet is a prudent thing to do—especially when he has a couple of little kids running around the house. It's just plain stupid. Any dog can be aggressive, but these dogs are so powerful they have the potential to kill.

Sure, you can raise a Rottweiler to be docile, but what's going to happen when something goes wrong? When this dog gets old and crotchety and his brain chemistry goes completely haywire, he'll turn on somebody. And then what? Congratulations. You'll live the rest of your life knowing that your dog killed a neighborhood 4-year-old. To my way of thinking, that's just plain ridiculous.

You want to own a dog that's a deadly weapon? Then, by God, you should do what Ralph does: Get your dog a metal collar and have it chained to a *QE II* anchor that's bolted into bedrock, and make sure your property is plastered with signs that say things like "Survivors Will Be Prosecuted."

Ray's Law: Your Dog Is Your Agent

I can only assume that people who buy dogs like Rottweilers, pit bulls, and the like get a certain thrill from having a dog that is powerful and threatening. I don't have a problem with that. This is America, and it's a free country. But I think the law should be as follows: If you allow your dog to do something stupid, the law should view your dog as your agent.

In other words, these irresponsible dog owners deserve to be treated as if *they* had committed the crime themselves, nothing less.

Now, don't get me wrong. We all know that every dog has the potential to bite. Take, for example, my neighbor's

Lhasa apso. Sure, even that little dog can bite. On a good day, if he was really, really mad, he might very well be able to do in your pet parakeet. In fact, sometimes it seems like it's the littlest dogs that are most apt to bite. It's the little dogs that believe in the preemptive strike. (Hey, if I weighed 12 pounds, I'd feel that way too! At that weight you don't get a second chance.)

But the Lhasa apsos of the world aren't likely to kill anybody. If you have a dog that's a barker or maybe a little bit aggressive, fine. If he bites someone, then, sure, you might get sued. But at least you're not going to have it on your conscience that one of the neighbor's kids died because your 165-pound "best friend" had him for hors d'oeuvres. Dogs like Rottweilers and pit bulls have the potential to kill with little or no provocation, especially when their owners have trained them to be aggressive and protective. That's what disturbs me about them.

I have a dog. She's a Border collie. She's never bitten anyone I know. (She hasn't bitten anyone I don't know, for that matter.) Philly's certainly had confrontations with other dogs, in which she has snarled and bared her teeth. But I never worry that she's going to take down one of the neighbor's kids for a snack.

Smith & Wesson vs. Brutus

Owning a pit bull or a Rottweiler is no different, in my opinion, than having your 5-year-old find a loaded gun in a kitchen drawer and shoot the kid next door. You'd be criminally responsible for that lapse in judgment. The same laws should apply for these dogs. Your dog gets out of the yard and attacks somebody? Somebody comes into your yard when it's not properly posted, and he gets chewed into hamburger? You're guilty. And you go to jail. Or maybe we feed you to the dogs and you see how it feels!

I think it's ridiculous that people want to defend themselves with a dog. If you want to defend yourself, go buy a gun. At least you have more control over the gun. If you don't want to use it, you can lock it up. You don't have to feed it and it won't crap on the living room carpet.

Some owners who buy these dogs and train them to be vicious end up experiencing an ironic turn of events. They lose a loved one to the very dog that's supposed to be "protecting" them. Thanks, I feel better now.

Half-Baked Science

(Ray)

For the record, I would like to state the following: I think the global warming "crisis" is utter bull feathers.

There, I've said it. Want to take a guess on how many scientists who are currently working on global warming actually believe it's a problem or even fixable? It's only about 30%.* So, you may ask, whom do we have to blame for this hysteria? Well, that 30% and maybe Al Gore, the father of the Internet.

A few years ago, the scientific community approached the world leaders and said, "Look, we've got a problem

---

* This may be complete BS. I made it up. There is absolutely no statistical or scientific evidence to support this claim or any of the scientific principles put forth in this essay. You are, however, free to believe anything you wish.

with chlorofluorocarbons getting into the upper atmosphere and eating away at the ozone layer." Where do these chlorofluorocarbons come from? Well, one place they come from is refrigerants, like R12. So we have to ban R12 and come up with a new refrigerant that won't damage the ozone layer. And we'll begin to use this in all the cars and all the air-conditioning systems all over the world. And we have to ban aerosol cans that use chlorofluorocarbons as a propellant, because that's getting into the atmosphere, too. Well, I just don't buy it. They don't mention the fact that the chlorine from these chlorofluorocarbons that's wrecking the ozone layer is overshadowed tremendously by the amount of chlorine introduced into the atmosphere every day by volcanoes. We have no control over volcanoes. And as far as I know, we never have. What are we going to do? Ban volcanoes? OK, we're going to cap all the volcanoes. We'll outlaw volcanoes. No more volcanic action on the planet, and we'll have no more chlorine going into the atmosphere.

Now I know some scientists say, "Well, that chlorine that's coming out of those volcanoes, that's just CL_2 and not a danger to the ozone layer." Well, I believe that enough of that chlorine comes out as free-radical chlorine (CL-minus), and that's the very stuff they claim is doing the damage. Well, if that's doing the damage, then banning spray cans of Right Guard isn't going to help very much, because the chlorine of volcanic origin is bajillions of times greater than the amount of chlorine that's coming out of our spray deodorant cans.

Now, don't get me wrong, there are lots of good reasons, perhaps, to ban things, but I'm just afraid that our replacement for chlorofluorocarbons may turn out in years to come to be even more of a threat to mankind than the stuff it replaced. The jury's still out on that. We'll see. Now, if we really want to ban something, I'd like to suggest that we consider cows. This may be news to some of you, but bovine flatulence, which is mostly methane, is believed by some scientists to be another leading cause of global warming. Geez!

I guess we humans just find it hard to accept the fact that there are certain ecological and environmental factors beyond our control. Let's not forget that the planet had gone through cycles of warming and cooling long before mankind was here to screw up the environment, and what caused those? We don't know. There are forces at work that are so complex we can't possibly understand them, and even if we could, we certainly couldn't control them. Let's not let the scientific community lead us astray. The problem with science is scientists. For the most part, they're intelligent, they're articulate, and they're convincing. Furthermore they don't seem to be in it for the money. So when they tell us something, we believe it because they've been studying this subject and we haven't. And everyone wants to believe in something. Everyone wants someone to give him the answer. The scientists always seem to have the answers.

And is it any surprise that most of our prominent, or at least most vocal, scientists are men? Men have answers for all the questions, and many of those answers have been proven wrong throughout history. Let's look at a few examples. One of the earliest, and maybe even greatest, scientists of the ancient world was Aristotle. He had everyone believing that Earth was the center of the universe and that everything revolved around our planet. Hmm. Guess we found that wasn't true, but mankind believed it for a long, long time. I think something like 15 centuries. Let's not forget how many scientists had everyone convinced that the earth was flat.

Here's one of my personal favorites, and I think this has been in just about every science book that I've ever read. Heat radiating from the earth's core is the result of a long-term cooling process that started when the earth was a molten mass. Remember this one? We were taught that the heat from the core of the earth was created at the earth's beginning and has been slowly released ever since. I don't believe it. I don't give a damn how high an R value our planet has, after 4 billion years, the core of the earth should have cooled off completely. I don't think you need a Ph.D. to figure that out. I think scientists now know, after foisting this harebrained theory on us for years, that this is complete nonsense. There is—there must be, a nuclear reaction taking place at the center of our planet, and probably every planet that is something more than a frozen glob of interstellar rock. And yet the scientific community had us believing that this was, in fact, the absolute truth and it was not to be disputed. And now we know the truth; it's baloney. I mean, come on, we know that there is radioactivity all through the planet, and this radioactivity is what's keeping the core of the earth molten, not heat that was trapped in there 4.2 billion years ago. Let's get serious.

Here's another one I love. Imagine how many dinosaurs it would take, standing shoulder to shoulder in a place like Saudi Arabia, just so those Saudis could pump 9 billion gallons of oil out of the ground every 10 minutes. It's just impossible. The truth is, there is no such thing as "fossil" fuel. We were taught in school that we get oil out of the ground because billions and billions of dinosaurs all decided to die in the same place and were then covered up by rock and dust and falling trees, and under tremendous pressure over millions and millions of years those decaying dinosaurs turned into oil! We all fell for that one. What we do know is that geologists have found oil in certain places on Earth where they know dinosaurs never existed. Splain me that, Lucy. A more reasonable explanation is that oil is constantly being manufactured from the elemental components of the earth. Carbon and hydrogen atoms, trapped beneath the earth's crust, are being combined by the heat generated from that aforementioned molten mass of 4.2 billion years ago. That's where oil comes from—in my humble opinion. Now if you really believe that oil came from decomposing pterodactyl wings, you know what? We should have run out about 112 years ago.

So what's my point? Well, I'm glad you asked. I propose that we're just too quick to accept what the scientific community is telling us. We figure they must be telling us the truth because they've explained so many things correctly in the past and they don't seem to be trying to sell us something. When someone is trying to sell you a vacuum cleaner, you know he's lying because he's in it for the money. But the scientific community seems to be above that, and therefore we've made the mistake of elevating scientists to the level of gods. Why? Because they explain the things to us that we can't explain to ourselves. And you know what? We're too quick to believe them, if only because they always sound like they know what they're talking about. And they look like they know what they're talking about, too. They've got that wild hair and that wide stare and all those college degrees. They just can't be wrong. (By the way, don't believe me either, even if I sound like I know what I'm talking about.) It's high time we stopped believing all these bogus theories that a bunch of half-baked scientists are spoon-feeding us.

Look at it this way—even if all the doomsayers are right about global warming, so what? There was an article in the *Boston Globe* (the major newspaper in Our Fair City) last year about life on our planet just after the last ice age. (By the way, what caused that ice age, anyway? We don't know.) In any event, scientists say that after that ice age, temperatures in some parts of the planet rose 19 degrees in just a few decades. Well, I don't believe that either, because I don't believe they have the means to really measure that. But let's assume for the time being that it's true. How did that happen? And wouldn't that have seriously altered any life that was on the planet at that time? Well, it certainly did, and that's part of the process; life on Earth gets altered by climatic changes. And certainly life, as we know it now, will get altered by global warming. And when it does, we will not have caused it; it's part of the ever-changing nature of planet Earth. We've simply attached too much importance to our impact on this giant planet. Let's get serious. Now, I don't know where you're living, but another 19 degrees in Boston would look just about perfect to me. That's my opinion. I'm probably wrong, but I'm sticking with it.

Stop the World— I Wanna Get Off!: The Other Side of Road Rage

(Tom)

It seems that everywhere I turn, the world is getting worse and worse—more and more hopeless. Now it's road rage. I can't believe the aggressiveness, the rudeness, the complete lack of civility and consideration I hear about. For example, motorists in New York City refuse to pull over for an ambulance. An ambulance! Imagine it—here is an emergency vehicle taking a dying person to a hospital, and some downtown stockbroker thinks his meeting is more important. Give me a break! Again, in New York, some guy shoots a woman who cut him off in traffic. Shoots her! Kills her! In Boston, drivers routinely refuse to come to the mandatory stop for school buses. A kid gets hit practically every week because some absolutely moronic jerk has to get to work on time. Stop the world, guys—I want off. There's no hope. It's gone too far.

At least that's what the media would have us believe. I've seen road rage on TV specials, read all the newspaper and newsmagazine articles, listened to all the talk shows. They all conclude that the reasons for this behavior are so deep-rooted in our warped psyches that (1) it's hopeless and (2) we should *definitely* not try to do anything about it, lest we become victims of the madness.

Well, on reconsideration, don't bother to stop the world, because I realize I've got nowhere else to go. So, we better fix the world we have. And, personally, I'm mad as hell and I ain't gonna take it anymore. The reason we're paralyzed is that we see the perpetrators as an amorphous mass of millions of unidentified motorists.

What can any one of us possibly do? I know what I'd like to do. Take, for example, that bimbo who was tailgating me all the way down Route I-93 this morning at 65 mph. I wanted to stop her, pull her out of her big, fancy sport utility vehicle, and give her the dope slap she so justly deserved. I wanted to tell her how rude it is to creep up someone's backside because he's driving only 10 mph over the speed limit and that's not fast enough for her. I wanted to ask if her mother ever taught her any damn manners. And I wanted to put an UNremovable bumper sticker on her back fender that said I AM AN UNMITIGATED RUDE JERK AND I DESERVE WHATEVER I GET.

God, I wanted to do that. But I didn't.

But doesn't someone have to do it? If no one does, won't she and others of her ilk take over the world? Won't *they* determine what's right? Do I want people like her determining the standards of acceptable public behavior?

So, who's gonna do it? How about this—the people we

pay to do it? Yeah—the police. I know, I know—the police can't be everywhere. But can't they be somewhere?

On Route 128, the beltway around Boston, the police could, if they wanted to, issue 100,000 citations a day for speeding and tailgating. Instead, they are conspicuously absent during rush hours. By their absence, they are condoning—and reinforcing—illegal and uncivil behavior. Don't tell me that they don't *know* 100,000 drivers are speeding and tailgating every day. They know, but they don't want to disrupt rush-hour traffic!

Good thinking, boys.

I blame the police for every road rage confrontation because they never tell anyone their behavior is wrong. I blame them for every highway fatality because they never stop the people who drive recklessly. I blame them for my anger, my distress, my pain and suffering! (I also blame the Massachusetts Registry of Motor Vehicles—but that's another story.) Chances are, your state isn't much different.

You are the only one who can stop this blatant dereliction of duty. You are the one who must tell the police that you want them to do the job you pay them for. But you won't. And here's why. Because you're a coward. You know what's right. You know that, indirectly, every scofflaw is responsible sooner or later for the 1,000 people who die on the roads every week. And you know, in your heart, that you yourself are one of those scofflaws. But you don't want *your* license revoked. You don't want to take responsibility for anyone's death. Sure, you may drive too fast. Yes, you've tailgated to get the person in front of you to get on with it. You've blown the horn when someone hesitated for a nanosecond when the light turned green. And you may not really stop at every stop sign. But you're basically a nice person. You don't deserve to be punished for any of these minor infractions.

Great. Sleep tight. And pray it's not your kid who gets hit by the jerk passing the stopped school bus.

The Andy Letter

(Andy Reichsman, Intro by Tom)

No book of ours which purports to include philosophical musings would be complete without—as we refer to it—the Andy Letter. This letter has become the paradigm, the benchmark, the challenge for all those who seek fame and fortune. Here's a short introduction to the letter and a bit of the background (to which Andy alludes in his missive).

Whenever we meet people who know of us, they inevitably ask the following questions: "How do you manage to know all those answers? Do you have a computer in the studio? A staff of mechanics? Do you know the questions in advance and research the answers?"

Andy's letter will address the first question. And in so doing, you will discover that the answer to all the others is an unequivocal "no."

We got a call one day from some guy who had a brake

problem. We know brakes pretty well (it ain't rocket science), but this guy's problem was unique in that (1) The vehicle was a cattle carrier and (B) The brakes were electric.

Now we're a couple of city boys. We've never even seen cattle, never mind a cattle carrier. And neither of us had ever heard of electric brakes. But we couldn't send the guy away without at least an attempt at helping him. So, we asked a few questions (always helpful when you have no idea what the answer is) and we began to formulate hypotheses.

A few days later we got this letter from "Andy."

Dear Click and Clack,

I am writing to offer profound thanks to you for resolving an important philosophical question that has been heatedly debated for the last 20 years. The rumination began on a construction site one summer in the early 1970s, as my friend Jamie and I were working our way through college. The question we raised and have agonized over, lo these many years, is one that I've never read about in any philosophical treatise, and yet I have found it has applied to countless situations and conversations overheard in bars, repair shops, sporting events, political debates, etc.

Posit the question: Do 2 people who don't know what they are talking about know more or less than 1 person who doesn't know what he's talking about? (Pardon the un-PC use of the masculine pronoun, but I have found this to be predominantly a male phenomenon.)

In your recent conversation regarding electric brakes on a cattle carrier, I believe you definitely answered this query and have put our debate to rest.

Amazingly, you proved that even in a case where 1 person might know nothing about a subject, it is possible for 2 people to know even less!

One person will only go so far out on a limb in his construction of deeply hypothetical structures, and will often end with a shrug or a raising of hands to indicate the dismissability of his particular take on a subject. With 2 people, the intricacies, the gives-and-takes, the wherefores and why nots, can become a veritable pas de deux of breathtaking speculation, interwoven in such a way that apologies or gestures of doubt are rendered unnecessary.

I had always suspected this was the case, but no argument I could have built from my years of observation would have so satisfyingly closed the door on the subject as your performance on the cattle carrier call. To begin your comments by saying, "We'll answer your question if you tell us how electric brakes work" and "We've never heard of electric brakes," and then indulge in lengthy theoretical hypostulations on the whys and wherefores of the caller's problem, allowed me to observe that you were finally putting this gnarly question to rest.

I am forever indebted to you for the great service you have performed! I'm truly impressed that it took so many years of listening to your show to finally have this matter resolved.

Sincerely,

Andy R.

Bitch, Bitch, Bitch

(Tom)

For a long while, my brother lived his life according to the precepts of the renowned 20th-century philosopher Rooster Cogburn. Surely you've seen that great movie *True Grit*. Perhaps you never noticed that "The Duke" divulged his philosophy of life through brief one-liners uttered at appropriate—and exciting—moments. (One of my favorites is spoken when, in a drunken stupor, he falls off his horse. Picture it if you can. He's lying there on the ground, drunk as a skunk. The big tough guy. The leader of the small band in search of a murderer. In an attempt to salvage what little self-respect he may have—and to reestablish his leadership position—he looks up and says authoritatively, "We'll camp here.")

Here's another—in case you've never seen, nor wish to see, this Hollywood classic. Rooster's nemesis, Ned Pepper, has captured "the girl" (I don't remember who she was), and he's threatening to kill her if Rooster doesn't capitulate. They're yelling at each other across the western plains.

Ned hollers, "I've got the girl, Rooster. I'll have to kill her if . . ." (If something. I don't remember. It doesn't matter).

Rooster bellows in response, "You do what you think is best, Ned. The girl means nothing to me."

You do what you think is best.

Don't you love it?

Of course, it's all bravado. The girl is very dear to the old Rooster (but you knew that).

Anyway, you get the idea. Rooster had an aphorism a minute. My brother could quote you the script of the entire movie. (And he frequently did.) But my all-time favorite—I wish I could remember the context (I could ask my brother, but he'd probably say, "You do what you think is best, Tommy.")—is this one: "Enough is as good as a feast."

Not bad. And, I think, especially appropriate today.

Have you noticed that we've become a nation of crybabies? We expect everything to be perfect. (I blame this, to some extent, on the media and Hollywood. Ever seen a newscaster with a hair out of place? Even the "banter" between newscaster and weatherman is perfectly scripted. "Well, Bill, how does it look for the weekend?" "Glad you asked, Bruce." Oh, give us a break!)

Does everything always have to be perfect? And if it's not, can we whine? Instead of noticing how wonderful almost everything is, we focus on what isn't. (Have you heard the one—told to me by a Jewish friend—about the three little old Jewish ladies dining in a fancy restaurant. The waiter comes by, leans over, and asks, "Is anything all right?")

Next time you find yourself on the verge of whining, repeat the mantra: Enough is as good as a feast.

In the days when I was under the influence of Omean (see "Omean Aspiavodos"), I came to an interesting revelation. A formula for life—in the true sense of the word.

Happiness = Reality - Expectations.

Or, for you mathematical types, more correctly: Happiness = f(Reality - Expectations). I really don't know the shape of the functional relationship. I hope you're happy.

But let's keep it simple. Revelation or not, the formula just says that if your expectations are higher than reality, you have negative Happiness—which I think is not good. This leads to an interesting—in my humble opinion—conclusion: that the happiest people are cynics.

By outward appearances, optimists are the happiest people. Au contraire, piston puss. Optimists have high expectations—by definition. I mean, this is what optimists are—rosy outlook people. But reality hardly ever matches these high expectations. Do the math:

(Low) Reality - (High) Expectations = (Negative) Happiness.

Optimists are, therefore, almost always disappointed, and thus unhappy. They just won't admit it.

How about pessimists? They're unhappy, too. True, they have low expectations, but they have hope. Life sucks (they say to you), but maybe not this time (they say to themselves). This hope raises their expectations so that the equation again has a negative value.

—JOHN WAYNE aka ROOSTER COGBURN

We come to cynics. Cynics are the happiest. By outward appearances, they seem to be pessimists. They say the same kinds of things: Life sucks. But they truly believe it! That is, they have NO hope.

Let's do the math. To cynics, Reality is a big zero. But so are their Expectations! So

$$Happiness = 0 - 0 = Zero!$$

Not great, but better than negative. They win.

The Road to Happiness

Thanks to the media, we have become a nation of crybabies and whiners. We just ain't happy. Our personal Reality can never approach the Expectations of perfection required to be happy.

Reminds me of a great line from an old movie—I think it was *Lovers and Other Strangers*. The male lead, Richie, tells his mother that he wants to be happy. To which Mom responds, "Happy? Who's happy? You keep looking for happiness, Richie, it's going to make you miserable."

And now we know from our Happiness equation that the problem is high Expectations. And who comes to the rescue? Rooster Cogburn, who else?

Enough is as good as a feast.

A Man Can't Just Sit Around

(Peter Garrison, Intro by Tom)

When you read this brief account of Larry Walters, you'll realize the level of quiet desperation in your own miserable, uneventful life. You may be a successful professional—even a world-renowned scientist or poet. Hell, you could even be the Dalai Lama himself, and you'd be nothing compared to Larry Walters.

Here's the story, written by Peter Garrison, that appeared in *Flying* magazine.

You've heard of Rickenbacker and Lindbergh and Doolittle. You've heard of Yeager. But have you heard of Larry Walters? Probably not. Yet Walters—like another relatively unsung hero, the legendary D. B. Cooper—was made of that special stuff that separates aviation legends from the common run of folk.

In 1982, Walters, a truck driver by trade, bought a bunch

of weather balloons at a surplus store. He filled them with helium and tied them to a lawn chair. He provided himself with a two-way radio, a parachute, some jugs of water, and an air rifle, and then cut his conveyance loose from the bumper of his car, which was anchoring it to the ground.

Take a moment to imagine the thrill and terror of that ascent, transforming a man surrounded by the normal appurtenances of life—garden, house, SUV—into a speck floating in an infinite space. Had he rigged up some sort of seat belt? Did the chair tip and wobble? Did he call out to the antlike figures below? We don't know.

It is clear, however, that he violated FARs by passing through Los Angeles TCA without a transponder or a clearance. Two passing jetliners reported to controllers that they had seen a man with a gun seated in a deck chair at 11,000 feet. A helicopter went up to take a look.

Walters had planned to descend by shooting out the balloons with his pellet gun, one at a time. He had deflated 10 of them this way, when he accidentally dropped the gun. Evidently 10 was enough. After being carried out to sea and back on the vagrant coastal breezes, he was snagged by power lines in Long Beach, and led away in handcuffs. He is reported to have said, by way of explanation of his exploit, "Man can't just sit around."

Walters subsequently fell on hard times, became bankrupt, and died by his own hand in 1993. But his memory survives as a model of those qualities of independence, vision, and disregard for common caution without which aviation would never have come into being.

The Wacky Way of Knowledge

(Tom)

I am about to impart to you a small portion of the wisdom of the ages. I kid you not.

In a few minutes, you will be made aware of a theory so profound in its implications that it must—and will—change everything you have ever had the terrible misfortune to believe.

Reincarnation—a precept embraced by a very significant percentage of the world's population—proposes that we humans are the highest life-form on the planet. Further, they say, higher life-forms can exist—beyond merely average humans—and by following various paths, we can achieve the character, virtues, and happiness of these higher life-forms after death. I suppose that they claim that the "lower" life-forms—plants, animals, insects, etc.—are on their way to being reborn into human form—assuming that they live good lives as plants, animals or insects.

Boy, they're so close.

But I, L. Ron Tappet, will now reveal to you a counter-proposal—with a logic so unassailable that its truth will be immediately and compellingly apparent.

Although the theory of reincarnation is correct (as revealed to me by Omean Aspiavodos), the direction of nirvana—as it is understood by its current adherents—is bass ackwards. Humans—the highest form of life on the planet? As my brother would say, "Au contraire, piston puss." Quite the opposite. Look around. If reincarnation is supposed to produce better and better people, WHERE ARE THEY?

Where is the slightest evidence of the truth of this belief? War, murder, mayhem? Are these characteristics of a high life-form? I think not. In the next few paragraphs I will share with you the research on which the new theory of reincarnation is based—and the startling results.

The Genesis of the Theory

It's interesting how research happens.

One day one of us—I can't remember which one it was—came across a quotation from that great Hebrew philosopher Isaac . . . Newton. You may recall the quote. He said, "If I have accomplished anything in my life, it is because I have stood on the shoulders of giants." Wow! What a powerful thought. And humble. (I, too, am quite humble. In fact, I think that it is my humility which makes me so great.)

But after a few moments—after we'd had a chance to think about it a bit—we wondered, "Is it in fact true in all areas of endeavor that people accomplish great things because they stand on the shoulders of giants?"

So we tell Paul Murky, director of Murky Research—the research arm of Dewey, Cheetham and Howe—to study this. And he comes back to us with a couple of hypotheses:

The Null Hypothesis: Well, of course, it applies to all areas, all endeavors, because we humans have been on the planet for hundreds of thousands of years and we each benefit from whatever has been done by our predecessors. That's the "shoulders of giants" hypothesis.

The Alternative Hypothesis: "Oh yeah?" The alternative hypothesis is that it simply is not true. In some areas, yes, we do in fact benefit from what our predecessors have done (like science), but in other areas, mostly the human involvement kinds of areas, we may in fact all be destined to make the same mistakes over and over and over again, generation after generation, child after child. And so there is never any giant on whose shoulders you can stand, and therefore there is no progress.

So Murky starts to work, and as he will do, Murky doesn't stick strictly to what we asked him to do. One day we catch him (I think it's called) "mucking around in the data."

He comes to us and says, "Guys, I have been mucking around in the data. And I have a finding here that is going to knock your socks off."

Murky explains that since the null and alternative hypotheses basically involved left brain/right brain functions, he had used a standardized psychological battery of questions which included these as well as many other constructs—among them "Happiness." And while mucking around in the data, he discovered an interesting relationship. (See Figure 1.)

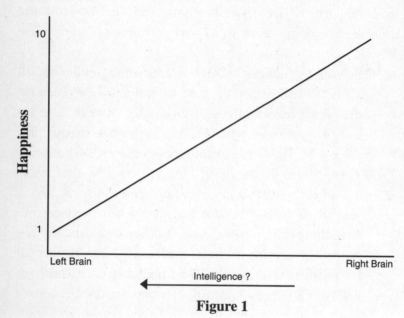

Figure 1

Murky had plotted happiness on one axis and the degree of left brainness and right brainness of the respondents on the other. (Of course, he had done a regression analysis and obtained an R-squared value of approximately 0.98. Pretty darn good, no?) The chart clearly shows that people with predominantly right brain strengths are 10 times as happy as those with strong left brain function. Wow! Doesn't that knock your socks off!?

Now keep in mind that left brain function is what some people think of as "intelligence." Ergo, the stupider you are (by left brain people's measures of stupidity), the happier you are!

We were flabbergasted! This was an awesome finding.

But as surprising and mind-boggling as this finding may be, it turned out to be only the beginning. The beginning of a theory of life so far-reaching that it changes all we know about civilization, humankind, and the cosmos itself. Get ready.

Like all good researchers, my brother and I decide to extrapolate. If dumb people are happier—we posit—let's test the theory with really dumb people. Murky is way ahead of us. "I've already thought of that," he says. "I included Harvard students in the sample. People don't get any dumber than that."

And then the breakthrough occurred. Raymond says, "People don't get any dumber than that, maybe. But why limit our research to people?"

Murky jumps with joy! "I can do it!" he screams. Murky claims that he can extend the research to other life-forms; and through a methodology which he will not reveal to us, he was indeed able to determine the happiness level of other life-forms. (This brings to mind one of Tom Lehrer's great lines, "He practiced animal husbandry—until they caught him at it.")

But I digress. Here are the results, which will truly knock your socks off. (See Figure 2.)

On the left, we have humans (and, as you will recall, the best of the humans are the right brain humans). With all other life-forms, happiness increases. The next happier life-form is a golden retriever. Then the cow. Then worms. Murky stopped his research at grass.

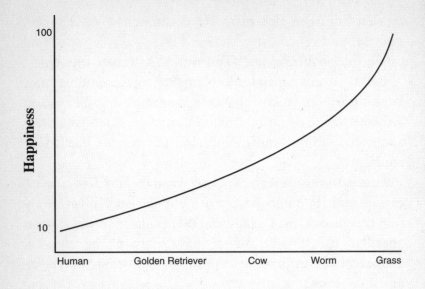

Figure 2

Ponder if you will, the importance of this.

Have you pondered? Good.

We have always thought that we humans are the highest life-form on the planet. Turns out, we are the lowest life-form. This finding leads us inexorably to a theorem which—as promised—changes everything we've ever believed.

[**ASIDE:** Some theories are just complete bullshit. Take, for example, the Big Bang Theory. Scientists would have us believe that The Entire Universe was once compacted into a dot. A DOT! It explodes. Why does it explode? Well, they don't know why. So they call it a "singularity." (Interpret as "None of this makes any sense, so please don't ask any embarrassing questions, or I'll have to make up more meaningless words".) Anyway, it explodes. And out of it come all the stars that you can see in the sky, all the planets, Rush Limbaugh, General Motors, the cheese steak. Give me a break. On the other hand, some theories, once posited, evoke "My God, of course that's true." You're way ahead of me, aren't you?

The Theory of Reverse Reincarnation

It's so obvious, isn't it? Animals don't come back as people. In fact, the facts suggest quite the opposite. Humans appear, by all measures, to be the lowest of life-forms! But look further. Do you see creatures on the planet which have, indeed, achieved nirvana? Creatures which do not kill? Creatures filled with love for all other creatures? People come back as animals, thus achieving greater and greater levels of happiness.

Think of cows, for example. Cows which follow "the path" (pun intended) will not be reincarnated as humans; on the contrary, humans will return as cows! Observe, if you have the opportunity, the peace and tranquillity of our bovine cousins. Does there exist a human of such tranquillity? I think not.

Follow Us, My Children, to Happiness

So, it becomes clear that the theory of reverse reincarnation may be the scientific finding of . . . not the decade, not the century, but of all time. Now, my brother and I, L. Ron, the Tappet Brothers, are going to help you achieve nirvana. We're going to help you to become not smarter. Smarter is no good. Getting smarter is the wrong direction. You are sliding down the happiness curve. You must stop this from happening, and you must go in the other direction. We are here to help you.

There is a process for reaching nirvana, and we are going to reveal it to you now. It is this: You must repeat the mantra. And the mantra is (in Latin, of course): *Non impediti ratione cogitationis*. (Unencumbered by the thought process.)

Repeat it aloud: *Unencumbered by the Thought Process*.
Again: *Unencumbered by the Thought Process*.
Louder: *Unencumbered by the Thought Process*.
Good.
Follow us, my children, to happiness.

THE FOUNDING
FATHERS

All forms of BIGOTRY are to be abhorred.

Except, of course, against the FRENCH.

— MARK TWAIN

The Founding Fathers: What a Bunch of Morons

(Tom)

Why Democracy Doesn't Work

You may sometimes wonder just whose idea this democracy thing was anyway. I do.

I mean, I've heard some really dumb ideas in my day, but this one ranks up there with the Big Bang Theory in terms of stupidity.

Think about it. You have a fairly large group of people who have decided to live together (or more likely they haven't decided any such thing. Circumstances have just plunked them down in close proximity to one another.). In any event, a few of them are intelligent enough to realize that they really ought to set down some ground rules in order to keep things somewhat harmonious.

Who should do that? I mean, who should set down the

rules? And—I ask you—what answer did they come up with? They came up with: "everyone." Yes, everyone should have a say in deciding what the ground rules will be. After all, aren't all men created equal? To the Founding Fathers, the stupidity of this idea was not immediately obvious. So, they decided to give it a try.

It mustn't have taken very long for a couple of truths to become abundantly clear:

1. It takes forever to decide anything. After all, everyone gets to express his opinion on everything! Nothing is getting done.

2. Some people are complete idiots; I mean, dumb as a brick. But we did say "everyone," didn't we? We didn't say everyone with an IQ higher than a brick, did we?

At this point you would think that at least one of the Founding Fathers would have had the good sense to see that they had made a little mistake here. Nay, a rather big mistake.

[ASIDE: Since writing this, I've learned that someone did indeed question this silly idea. Alexander Hamilton evidently asked Thomas Jefferson, "But what if the people are wrong?" I think Jefferson answered, "Let me get back to you on that."]

But did they admit the mistake? Did they attempt to "amend" the idea to include the IQ and the brick thing? No. Why not? Well, they had thought up the idea in the first place, so how could they admit that it had been a mistake?

3. They were all males. And admitting that they had

made a mistake would be tantamount to asking for directions. Out of the question.

So, they stick with their silly idea, and now *we* seem to be irrevocably stuck with it. It clearly isn't working—nor can it ever work—because, it's based on a false premise: All men are NOT created equal. They're just not. It ain't rocket science, folks.

It seems that you and I should have realized a long time ago that these Founding Fathers were a few sandwiches short of a picnic. I mean, think about some of their other great accomplishments. For example, it took these great men—and the "great men" who succeeded them—about 100 years to notice that what they had really meant was that all men are created equal, as long as their skin is white. Duh. And more than 100 years to notice that they had forgotten to mention women.

Given all of this, just who were these Founding Fathers, anyway, and why have we deified them? They appear to have been morons. Well, if we admit how stupid the average person is, the following thought comes to mind: In a land of idiots, a moron is a genius.

Now what?

Well, I have some suggestions. (But you knew I would, didn't you?) Here's what I think:

The Magliozzi Principle
Part 1

We need a Philosopher-King.
If the Founding Fathers had had any brains, they'd have

realized that among them there was maybe one person who really had it all together. One person whom they all trusted. That's the person who should have decided the ground rules. Not "everyone." Wouldn't you want a "wise man" deciding things rather than Clem Kadiddlehopper? This is a no-brainer.

Part 2

The largest group of people to be subjected to any one set of ground rules should never exceed about 500. This is the number at which a) the Philosopher-King can know everyone, and b) everyone can know the Philosopher-King—personally (not by a couple of televised sound bites selected by the media—another bunch of morons, in my humble opinion).

So, here's the deal. Start looking around for the other 499 people you'd like to live with. Make sure that among them is a candidate or two for Philosopher-King.

Start buying up the real estate where youse would like to live. Be creative.

You've got 18 months to reorganize. Good luck. If you need to get in touch, I'll be in Hawaii. If Pamela Anderson Lee answers, hang up.

NOTE: Of course I realize that the philosophy being promulgated here is not in agreement with that presented in "A Taxonomy of Humankind." Feel free to mix and match.

The Founding Fathers: Counter-Rant

(Ray)

When I found out that our publisher had decided to include Tommy's democracy rant in this book, I was dumbstruck. What were they thinking? I begged, I pleaded, but to no avail. So I immediately got to work on a counter-rant, afraid that our readers might get the wrong idea; the idea that we're both crazy. Now if he wants you to think he's crazy, that's OK, but leave me out.

So, let's look at this democracy thing. I'm sure my brother must have missed more than a few civics classes to have formed the belief that we live in a democracy. In a true democracy everyone has a say regarding all the goings-on in that society. Well, except for a few town meeting forms of government in rural America, or perhaps your bridge club, that's not the way our government works at all. Our Founding Fathers created a republican form of government, where indeed the people got to vote, but not on the individual issues or the laws. They got to vote instead for leaders, and it's those leaders whose job it is to enact the laws and ratify treaties, or appropriate money for new schools or bridges, etc., And sure enough, those Founding Fathers did eventually give every man, and every woman, a vote in the electoral process. Even complete idiots have a right to choose a leader.

But they certainly didn't give everybody a say about everything, as Tommy suggests; and I'm glad they didn't. Who would have enough time for all that decision making? I know I wouldn't. I can't even decide what to wear in the morning. I'm glad we have elected officials; at least we can throw the bums out every few years if they're doing a lousy job. You're not going to get rid of any Philosopher-King that easily. That's a lifelong job. You'd have to kill the guy. Now, Tommy must have missed a few history classes as well, because these 500-person little kingdoms he proposes, I think have been tried before. In fact, they called it feudalism, and I'm sure if he thought about it a little more, he would have suggested walled enclaves, or maybe even castles with moats filled with alligators. Geez, what a nut! I'll keep our system of government, thank you!

Certainly our Founding Fathers made some obvious mistakes on our constitution, but they made provisions for amending it. In fact, they started amending it the day they finished it, and hopefully we'll continue to amend it. I know that our system seems terribly slow at times, and always subject to compromise, but that's good, too. It makes everyone feel that he's part of the process, and believe me, that's important. I think Tommy is ticked off because he thinks he's got great ideas, and he should be Philosopher-King. Yet nobody listens to him. Why? Well, honestly, most of his ideas are . . . well, wacky. In fact, his wife and kids stopped listening to him years ago, and his dog listens only if he has a pork chop tied around his neck. But even the dog is making progress. He just learned to play dead.

DON'T LIE, CHEAT OR STEAL

—UNNECESSARILY

The Counter-Rant to the Counter-Rant

(Tom)

Boy, my dear brother sure has his head up his keester on this one. Democracy vs. republic? The right to elect leaders? Bah. Details, semantics. And you call these sleazeball politicians leaders? The system stinks. And what's this excuse about the system being a little slow and subject to compromise? I'll show you a prime example of so-called leaders and how they "compromise." You tell me if it doesn't smell to high heaven (almost literally—as you'll see).

A year or so ago, the U.S. Department of Agriculture decided to define the term "organic"—to protect us poor uneducated slobs so that we wouldn't be taken in by some unscrupulous retailers who might use the "organic" label on foods that don't really deserve it. So, they studied the issue for some months and then published their definition. Lo and behold, the definition included foods that are "irradiated, genetically engineered or grown with sewage sludge fertilizer."

Luckily, some people actually read the document—probably "real" organic farmers. They didn't like it. The USDA received 200,000 complaints.

Now, the story thus far is bad enough. But get this: when they receive the complaints, the agriculture secretary—a bureaucratic moron (in my opinion)—makes a statement. Here's what he says (and I paraphrase): "Gee, we didn't realize so many people would be upset by this. I guess we'll take another look." You didn't REALIZE that people would be upset by the words "irradiated," "genetically engineered," and "sewage sludge"? Who the heck are you trying to kid?

First of all, if it's true that you didn't realize the words "irradiated," "genetically engineered," and "sewage sludge" don't immediately leap to mind when we poor slobs think of "organic" foods, then turn in your resignation immediately. Do not pass GO and certainly do not collect another paycheck.

Second, we don't believe that you didn't know. What we do believe is that you were influenced—legally or illegally—by vested interests. (I don't know how to check on this, but I'd bet the remains of my dear departed Dodge Dart that lobbyists from the irradiation, genetic engineering, and sludge businesses made lots of calls and bought lots of lunches for the USDA that year—in my opinion.)

Now tell me that doesn't stink to high heaven. And it's just one small example of what goes on every single day.

Here's my point. Our rants have frequently focused on truth, justice, and the American way—and especially on why there is so little truth or justice in the American way.

One has to ask, What is the good of this right to vote? Why do we have a Congress—or any elected officials, for that matter? It's a farce. The way I see it, rich, powerful businesses and rich, powerful individuals give tons of money to the elected officials, who in turn appoint their buddies to important positions—like Agriculture Secretary. Then the elected officials—and their appointed buddies— do what the rich, powerful businesses and individuals want them to do.

Of course, I have a suggestion for correcting all this. If you don't like the idea of a Philosopher-King, let's not waste our valuable time with elected officials. We have better things to do. I might even get a haircut.

Since the elected officials are a big waste of time anyway, why not let the lobbyists run the country directly? Cut out the middleman. It would be much less expensive for every-body—and more honest.

In my humble opinion.

TIME IS MORE

IMPORTANT

THAN MONEY;

Time is more important than money;

YOU CAN

You can always acquire more money.

ALWAYS

ACQUIRE

MORE MONEY.

THE EDUCATION TRILOGY:
In Four Parts

Introduction

(Tom)

This is an introduction to 3 essays plus an epilogue on the one subject in the world that I think I know something about—education. (I know a little about cars—but not much compared to what I think I know about education.)

I've been an "educator" of one kind or another for over 30 years. I even have credentials—which in my opinion have contributed absolutely nothing to my knowledge of teaching and learning. (I suspect that most such education "credentials" have about the same worth; zero.)

I started teaching very soon after I graduated from college. First I tutored kids in math, and then I put together a series of courses to prep kids for the dreaded SAT exams. Beyond that, I was a college professor for about 30 years, at first on a part-time basis and then, in order to fulfill my "life dream" of being a real (i.e., full time) prof, I spent 9 years of my life getting a Ph.D.

Like many so-called educators, I was extraordinarily conscientious. I spent nearly every waking hour attempting to find new ways to make the esoteric subjects I was teaching more interesting and understandable. I was an unqualified success. Until I realized what a fool I had been.

Here's the problem. I had become so enamored of the challenges of teaching that I had forgotten a Great Unyielding Truth that I had long ago scribbled on a scrap of paper. It hung in my office and moved around as my office moved around. Here's what it said:

> It's more important to think about what
> you're doing than it is to do it.

I had spent over 30 years of my life believing that I was doing God's work (and devising better and better ways to do it), but I had never *really* thought about what I was doing. I had even taught courses about this error. In business schools, it's called local suboptimization. (Don't you just love expressions like this? I did, too.) It means you got a perfectly right answer, but you asked the wrong question.

The Trilogy

(Tom)

There are four parts to this trilogy:

Part I: The Allegory of the Epiphany at the Fountain, in which the Philosopher-King discovers the first question: Why do schools teach what they teach? (Which is wrong-headed. Completely wrong-headed!)

Part II: A Scathing Indictment, in which the Philosopher-King scathily indicts just about anyone remotely associated with education. And proposes what should be taught (instead of the crap discussed in Part I).

Part III: A New Theory of Learning, which ain't a theory and ain't so new. But so-called educators don't seem to have a clue. This one addresses not "what" we should teach, but "how" we should teach.

Part I: The Epilogue, in which the P-K tries to gather up all the loose ends that he forgot to mention in the other 3 parts.

Whether you agree or not, I hope you find it interesting. And, like all rants—as you may have guessed—I'm hoping it starts a revolution. I'd love to get your feedback on the Trilogy. Please write to me in care of the publisher or e-mail me at Tom@Cartalk.com.

Thanks for listening.

Part I: The Allegory of the Epiphany at the Fountain

Despite the fact that all of my being wanted to cry out in despair, I sat there quietly in my son's math class. It was "back to school" night—when parents get to spend 15 minutes in each of their kid's classes while "Teach" describes what the course is all about. On the board was the following description: "Calculus is the collection of techniques that allow us to determine the slope at any point on a curve and the area under that curve."

And all of my being wanted to cry out, "So who in God's creation gives a rat's patootie?" It took all of the self-restraint I could muster to keep my mouth shut. If you have a few minutes, I'll tell you why I was so distraught.

The Allegory of the Epiphany at the Fountain

Sometimes simple events have the power to provoke deep thoughts. Here's an example.

I've always wanted a fountain in my backyard. (I'm Italian. Or is that redundant?) Finally, this past summer, my dream came true. I thought I had died and gone to heaven. The sound of the water cascading from the mouths of four lions was more than I had ever hoped for. I sat beside my dream for hours, basking in the perfection of my peaceful reveries.

One day my lovely wife says to me, "Hey! Wake up! I've been thinking. The fountain doesn't look quite right just sitting there. I think it needs something around the base to set it off from the rest of the yard."

"Like what?" says I.

"Oh, I don't know. Maybe those cute Italian tiles (Italian? I perked up.) that I saw in one of my garden catalogs. Maybe a border of Italian tiles around the base would be nice."

The tiles were a great idea, thought I. (After all, they're Italian. I'm Italian, too. Did I mention that?)

So we decide to do the tiles. But it turns out not to be that simple.

Now, I should explain that the fountain has a narrow base upon which sits a large octagonal cistern into which the water flows as it exits the mouths of the aforementioned magnificent lions. My darling wife explained to me that she doesn't want the tiles to be directly under the cistern but rather 8 or 10 inches away from it, so we can have some room to plant some flowers; i.e., the tiles should form another octagon larger than the cistern octagon.

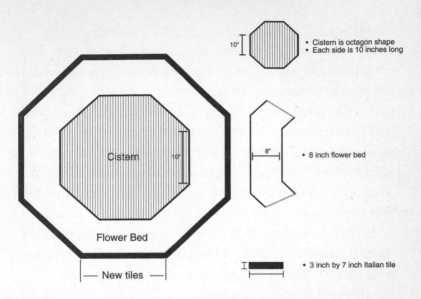

- Cistern is octagon shape
- Each side is 10 inches long

- 8 inch flower bed

- 3 inch by 7 inch Italian tile

Figure 3

Here's the problem: Are the tiles the right size? They come in only one size, 3 inches by 7 inches. The sides of the octagon of the fountain are 10 inches. If we put two tiles side by side, the new octagon will have to be 14 inches on a side.

Is this OK? That is, if we build a new octagon about 8 or 10 inches away from the fountain, will the sides be 14 inches?

"Hmmm," says I. "This appears to be a geometry/trigonometry problem. Boy, oh boy."

So, I sketch out the problem on the back of an envelope and proceed to do the necessary calculations (involving similar triangles and, of course, the theorem of Pythagoras). I conclude that if I build the new octagon 8 inches away from the base, the sides of the new octagon will be 14.4 inches. I.e., the tiles were perfect!

Wow!

This was the simple event that provoked what I think is an epiphany of sorts. There I was, sitting in my backyard solving an innocuous little geometry problem when it occurred to me that this was maybe the second time in my life—maybe the first—that I had had occasion to USE the geometry that I had learned in high school.

And, I had NEVER had occasion to use the higher mathematics that the high school math had prepared me for. *Never!*

Here's the revelation. Why did I—and millions of other students —spend valuable educational hours learning something that we would never use?

Is this education? Learning skills that we will never need? And even when I did get to use it, what did I use it for? To determine whether the 7-inch tiles would work at the base of my fountain. A problem, I might add, which I could have solved by cutting out a few 7-inch pieces of cardboard. And I might further add that it would have been faster with the cutouts.

Now to the larger issue. A while ago, I wrote a short rant about education for our Web site and created an Education Forum, in which I—using the tact and diplomacy for which I am well known—stated, "The entire educational system in this country stinks (pretty much). The people who run the education business are money-grubbing, self-serving morons." (C'mon, Tom, tell us what you really think.)

"The people who do the teaching are—for the most part—egomaniacs who don't have the faintest idea of what education should be all about." (I mean, do we learn by having some self-important jerk stand at the front of the room and attempt to "impress" us with everything he knows? It's well known that one's attention span under this scenario is about 20 minutes. Yet classes in high school are an hour long. In the MBA programs in which I taught for almost 20 years, classes were 3 hours long!)

"Clearly, the schools and colleges have no clue.

"So, let's figure it out for ourselves and fix it."

As I thought about my "fountain epiphany," I concluded that I had been wrong. It wasn't true that this event had been the first instance of an actual use of high school math before. I HAD indeed used that high school math before. I had used it as preparation for all the other math courses—including those I had taken at my good old alma mater, MIT. I had never used that math for any useful purpose! (And don't forget, I went to MIT. I was educated to be an engineer. I worked as an engineer for many years. And even at that, I had NEVER, ever had a need for these math courses.)

What about all those people who majored in art history? Or accounting? Or just about anything? Why had they all been subjected to "Calculus . . . the collection of techniques . . . blah, blah, blah?"

Here's my conclusion. The purpose of learning math, which most of us will never use, is only to prepare us for further math courses—which we will use even less frequently than never.

The answer I suppose I would get from math instructors is this: "You may never need it, but it teaches you to think."

You mean to tell me that there aren't enough "useful"

subjects that could be used to teach me to think? For example, I wish I had learned about decision trees in high school. Decision trees taught me to think. Decision trees are useful. Geometry is not. I wish I had learned about the real psychological and hormonal differences between males and females when I was in high school. That would have been really useful. Geometry is not. I wish I had learned about statistics and probability in high school, so that I could have been able to distinguish between truth and twisted truth. That would have been useful. Geometry is not.

So, why do schools teach geometry? Because they just don't understand what their job is; i.e., they are staffed by a bunch of megalomaniacs who know very little about teaching and learning. They teach it because "We've always taught it." These people are taking up my kids' valuable time, filling them with stuff they will never use—when there's SO much useful stuff they could be doing.

Tell me this isn't crazy.

Part II:
A Scathing
Indictment

As I said earlier, here's where I'm starting from: The entire educational system in this country stinks (pretty much). The people who run the education business are money-grubbing or self-serving morons or both. (C'mon Tom, tell us what you really think.) The people who do the teaching are—for the most part—egomaniacs who don't have the faintest idea of what education should be all about. My 30-some years as a college professor/instructor/lecturer gave me some insight into the **"how"** of teaching, but the epiphany at the fountain (see Part I) made me realize that very little (and/or intelligent) thought has gone into the question of **"what"** should be taught.

The importance of the question is—as they used to say at my old alma mater—"intuitively obvious," and one would think that "educators" (or educational professionals, as they like to be called) would have given it some serious thought. Yet, the "answer" they came up with compels us to reach one of only two possible conclusions: Either they did not actually think about this question, in which case they are surely idiots, or if they did in fact think about it and gave us what we now have, then they are at best morons.

After reading this rant, see if you agree.

So, What Should Education Be?

If you were going to "educate" a person, how would you define "educate"? After all, we do spend tens, if not hundreds, of thousands of dollars per person on education. How should we be spending that money? I mean, what should our goals be? WHAT should we teach them?

As I've thought about this, I've come to realize that there are at least 2 aspects to education. One major branch is "vocational teaching," or training people in the skills necessary to get jobs (this applies to medicine as well as plumbing and carpentry).

ASIDE: Interestingly, the one profession for which there currently is not any form of vocational training is that of college professor. One gets a Ph.D. in something like mathematics, for example, and learns a lot about math, but never takes a single course in teaching. Yet, s/he is then "qualified" to teach. And we pay them. Aren't we stupid?

Anyway, in addition to vocational learning, there is "everything else." What should the "everything else" be? (Note: just because I've broken education into these two pieces does not mean that I am suggesting that they need be "taught" separately. Quite the contrary.)

It seems to me that schools primarily teach kids how to take tests (a skill one hardly uses in real life unless one is a contestant on a quiz show). Elementary school prepares kids for junior high; junior high prepares them for high school. So, the goal—if we can call it that—of schools is to prepare kids for more school. And then to help them score well on a test administered by some (by now, very rich) people in Princeton, New Jersey, so they can get into the college of their—or their parents'—choice, where they sometimes learn stuff that will help them to get a job. But mostly not. (The punch line, "Do you want fries with that?" just ain't funny for a lot of people.)

Here Are Some of My Thoughts

A few weeks after having my epiphany at the fountain, I sat in my driveway, lit up a cigar, and scribbled the following notes on a pad of paper. (My early thoughts were quite simplistic; but I had to start somewhere.)

An educated person . . .

> Knows about lots of things. (Boy, I thought, this is really stupid.)
> Has perspective, gained from a knowledge of history (a little better).
> Has an appreciation of art, music, etc. (I decided that this was a "cultured" person. The same thing? I don't think so.)

Is always learning.
Understands the relative importance of things.
Understands himself.
Understands human nature.

Then I changed my approach.

An Education should prepare a person to . . .

Understand the world (includes government, politics, advertising, house construction, money, etc. This is a long list. Well, it's a big complicated world).
Make good decisions.
Know how to find answers.
Understand the relationships of things.
Love.
Care.
Have empathy.
Not be selfish.
See opportunities.
Communicate (includes languages and probably much more).
Understand what makes sense and what doesn't.
Appreciate beauty.
Have self-confidence.
Feel good about himself/herself.

Then I made a list of subjects I thought should be included in one's education:

Poverty.

Prejudice.

The cosmos.

Philosophies/religions.

How things work (cars, houses, your body, politics, advertising, cities).

Kids.

Growth/evolution—how things change.

Love.

Beauty.

Stupidity.

Old age.

Pain and pleasure.

Publications (there are so many).

What works and what doesn't (e.g., in health, in arguments, in advertising, in politics).

Health care.

Current events (and how to distinguish between real events and the nonsense we see/hear/read on TV, radio, and newspapers/magazines—especially "news" magazines).

I ended up with these thoughts.

1. The "everything else" part of education ought, first, to help us understand the world we live in. As much of it as possible, including flora, fauna, cultures, governments, religions, things (buildings, sewer systems; you know—"things").

2. Then it ought to help us to cope with that world.

3. And in the process, it ought to help us become good, kind, empathetic people.

Education should be preparation for life—
not preparation for school!

I thought that this wasn't too bad for a half-hour's thinking. Was this covered in calculus—"the set of techniques by which we can determine the slope at any point on a curve and the area under the curve?" I don't think so. (Please add the sarcasm as you read that last sentence. Go ahead. Read it again with the sarcasm. I think it works best with emphasis on the word *think*. Try it. I don't *think* so. Thanks. The jerks deserve whatever we dish out.)

A year or so ago I posed this subject to the visitors to our Web site. The response was overwhelming.

Here's the gist of the responses:

1. Preparation for life, as opposed to preparation for college, is a powerful idea. Overwhelmingly, the mail said that the emphasis on a "classical" education (by which we mean the usual math, science, history, etc., delivered by lecturers, with the goal of passing a test) is an ill-conceived notion. To quote my good friend Alex K., "My education prepared me to be a 19th-century gentleman." (Alex is the "most educated" person I know—with degrees from Yale, Harvard, and Oxford! It doesn't get any more "classical" than that, yet he thinks it was not a good education—especially regarding preparation for life. Nor did most of those who responded.) There were some who made a case for a classical education—but the mail was at least 10 to 1 against it.

2. Some of the reasons given for something *other than* a classical education:

Such an education focuses on a very small percentage of students—those who happen to have the left brain skills required to listen, remember, and regurgitate. Yet nearly all curricula are aimed at them. And even if they are good at it, so what? What have they learned—other than how to be a 19th-century lady or gentleman? And what about all the others of us who have some of the other "basic intelligences" described by Howard Gardner? (If you haven't read his stuff, go and buy everything he's written. You'll love it.)

3. There was tremendous support for this thought: "Of all the students in colleges today, a very large number should not be there." They are not interested in what's going on there—except for the social life. Yes, college does offer a venue for the very necessary socialization process of 18-to-22-year-olds. But let's admit that many colleges do little else FOR MOST OF THEM—excepting perhaps the 10 percent or so of students who are indeed motivated. A very large percentage of college students have little idea of how they could or should best spend the rest of their lives. Would you entrust the rest of your life to the decision of a snot-nosed 18-year-old kid? Me neither.

Sadly, most college curricula are ineffective and inefficient at helping anyone to decide what to do with his/her life.

Admittedly, 18-year-olds are not ready for the world. But might there not be better ways to help them that might be a little less expensive than the $30,000 per year that we're spending now? Must they socialize in multimillion-dollar chemistry labs?

4. Here's an idea from my brother—and, surprisingly, it's a pretty good one. He says to me, "You know, school departments are always underfunded. That's because they get their money from taxes. Schools should be funded BY INDUSTRY!" Then, just a few days later, there's an article in the *New York Times Magazine* (Sunday, July 5, 1998) about a very successful alternative school. And where do they get their money? From Honda!

I got one letter from a college dean who opened with "I think you're a little hard on teachers and the educational system. We're not perfect, but to condemn millions of teachers just because of a few hundred thousand rotten apples seems a bit extreme." But he did introduce me to writings of S.I. Hayakawa—specifically, "The Goals of Education," from *Through the Communications Barrier* (Harper & Row, 1979). Incidentally, it appears that this Hayakawa guy has stolen many of my ideas. How he did this 20 years before I wrote them down, I don't know.

A Sort of Interim Summary

So, what do you think?

Why are the schools teaching kids to take tests instead of preparing them for life? And what are tests for, anyway? To see if some (small) percentage of kids can remember and regurgitate? While intimidating all the rest? What about the self-esteem of the kids? Isn't that more important?

ASIDE: I once watched a live interview with W. Edwards Deming. (He's the guy who tried to show the U.S. auto industry what they were doing wrong. They wouldn't listen, so he went to Japan. They listened.) Someone asked Deming about testing. He thought for a moment—maybe trying to be tactful—and said, "Tests are useless." But how, they asked, will we know if the kids have learned anything? He said, "THEY'LL know."

Are the tests more to show how smart the teacher is? We KNOW that teachers know more than the kids. For one thing, they have the teachers' manual! And they've read it 50 times!

Why are schools teaching subjects that hardly anyone will ever use?

Why are college kids taking (required) courses? Who are colleges to say what our kids should study? If the kids don't know, how the hell do the colleges know?

We've been duped, my friends. And we know that if it's to be fixed, we have to do it ourselves. (The millions of home-schooling parents know this. Their kids learn to read and write—and they're a lot happier.)

(**NOTE:** Looking ahead, I realized that if such radical change in education is to take place, the people currently in charge are not going to do it. They have too much of a vested interest. For example, most people who are now teachers will be out of a job; no more boring trigonometry classes. No more memorization of state capitals. Whatever will they do? Repeat after me: "Do you want fries with that?")

Part III: The New Theory of Learning

The theory derives from many years of teaching experience. Nearly all of this teaching has been to MBA candidates. But since I wrote this, I've been noticing how even little kids learn, and I'm more and more convinced that the New Theory may apply at ALL levels of learning.

Premise I. The Little Red Schoolhouse Fallacy

I was a college professor for decades, during which time I became convinced that education had not progressed much beyond the Little Red Schoolhouse theory of learning: we put an expert in a roomful of people, and the expert proceeds to tell them everything he knows.

A major problem with this approach is that we ask people to sit and listen for long periods of time. Studies indicate that under such circumstances, we have an attention span of 20–30 minutes, and we retain about 20 percent of what we hear. This "teaching" doesn't result in much learning. It results in, maybe, someone remembering enough to pass a test. It's not learning. It's passing a test. You walk away from the test, and the valve in your brain opens and POOF—out goes the information to make room for the subject of the next test. An old Chinese proverb offers some guidance here:

> Tell me, and I will surely forget.
> Show me, and I might remember.
> Make me do it, and I will certainly understand.

Listening does not lead to understanding; doing does lead to understanding. Does the cobbler teach his son how to cobble by telling him about it? Does the doctor learn to perform appendectomies by reading about them? No. They DO IT.

From my own personal experience, doing something does lead to more learning. Perhaps your experience bears this out as well.

So, the first element of the New Theory is that students must "do" as opposed to sitting and listening.

Premise II: Only Real Reality Is Reality

Of course, there are various teaching methods that allow "doing" (for example, in MBA programs we use cases and term projects). A word about cases (which I used for near-ly all my years of teaching). The MBA case is an attempt to make the student "do it." But it's a somewhat feeble attempt. First of all, because the student very soon learns how to analyze cases and to feed back to the instructor what s/he knows the instructor wants to hear. Second, cases very soon get boring. Cases are dead, flat pieces of paper. They are an attempt to bring reality into the classroom, but they fail because they are very poor substitutes for real real-ity. The medical intern may spend some time on cadavers, but would you want a doctor trained on cadavers to oper-ate on your heart? Me neither.

The second element of the New Theory, then, is this: If you're going to DO it, you must do it with real people and real things in real situations.

Some may argue against this part of the theory on the fol-lowing grounds: "What happens to the syllabus?" "How can one predict that the real situation will offer all the opportunities for subject matter that the expert deems nec-essary for this course?"

The answer is that you can't predict that it will. In fact, you can be pretty damned sure it won't. It will offer far more! One of the benefits of REAL reality teaching is that it becomes—of necessity—multidisciplinary. You hardly ever encounter issues that all "fit" into one course. In MBA programs, for example, nearly all problems involve everything: marketing, finance, organizational behavior, operations research. You CAN'T isolate anything. Everything depends on everything else. (Yes, I know that there are multidisciplinary courses; but they are still not real.)

Premise III: The Backward Learning Theory

Here's a critical issue. People in the Little Red Schoolhouse environment have little (or no) idea of why they should want to know what the expert knows. In essence, we give them answers before they can really understand what the questions are. Sometimes, we tell them what the questions are. But mostly, they have no real *understanding* of the relevance of the questions to their lives. Example: "Now I'm going to teach you how to read financial statements." They ask, "Why would I want to know that?" No matter how we answer, they interpret it as "Because you will then be able to pass the exam I'm going to give you—and maybe get a higher-paying job." This is supposed to motivate people to want to learn. It doesn't. The motivation literature is very clear on this point. It tells us that real motivation doesn't derive from external rewards (like money or grades) but from intrinsic rewards (wanting to know and deriving satisfaction from, for example, solving a problem—the solution of which can lead to a real and short-term benefit to you). Our current techniques motivate students to struggle to remember enough to pass an exam.

Question: Why are we trying to teach people who don't really want to learn?

Motivation is the key. Motivation is everything! Of course, we know that some people are self-motivated. They have a desire to learn everything and anything. We don't have to worry about them. But others (most!) need to know why they should listen to you or me. Most of the problem here is that people are in colleges who don't belong in colleges. How the heck can an 18-year-old kid know anything about anything—or, more important, care about anything—besides the opposite sex? We fill schools with kids wasting their parents' money and looking for a place to socialize. There are better, less expensive, and more productive ways to do that. But I digress.

Here's what I've noticed about the relationship between learning and motivation. Maybe you've noticed it, too. Have you ever been faced with a problem like any of the following? Maybe you're trying to decide how to deal with a particularly difficult person. Or maybe you're staring at a pile of numbers and you don't know what the hell it all means. Or you're trying to decide whether to invest some money in a company and you can't make sense of the financials. Or—whatever. It's a problem for which you WANT an answer.

Let's take the first example—a difficult person—just to follow through on what you might do. You simply don't understand why the person is behaving the way she is behaving. If you understood why, you might be able to figure out what to do. Faced with such a problem, you might seek out an expert—someone who understands people's behavior. He might give you some insights. He might suggest that the problem really isn't unique. Lots of people act this way under certain circumstances. YOU MIGHT NOTICE THAT IN SUCH A SITUATION YOU ARE LISTENING VERY INTENTLY. QUITE UNLIKE THE WAY YOU LISTEN IN A CLASSROOM. He, the expert, might even suggest some things you might read to find out more. You can't wait to get to the library. You find books, articles. You read.

Think about HOW you're reading in this situation. Is it the same way you used to read textbooks when you were a student? It sure as hell isn't. The difference is that you're INTERESTED in finding the answer. And you have a context into which to put what you read.

Think about it some more. What do you actually do in these situations? Do you read everything? No. You're looking for answers to specific questions. What happens is this. You look at a lot of books and articles until you find something that seems relevant. You read it. Something strikes a chord: maybe a word, maybe a theory, maybe a description of a certain personality type that matches the one you're dealing with. Now you go in search of more info on that personality type. You find more books. They lead you to more. And pretty soon, you know what to do and how to do it.

While all this was happening, how might you have felt? Were you saying to yourself, "God, I wish I didn't have to read all this?" Did you yawn a lot? Did you ask, "Why am I reading this?" Hell, no. You probably wished you had more to read. More people to answer your questions. You were—LEARNING!

Notice what happened. You worked backward. You started with the problem. A problem that you had a need or desire to solve. You started somewhere—either with an expert or a book—and you went wherever it took you. And you went more than willingly; not with someone dragging you, kicking and screaming. You went because you wanted to go. Because you knew it was taking you where you wanted to go. Was there a syllabus? No. Did you need one? No. Did you cover everything that would have been in a syllabus? No. So what? When you need more, you'll learn it the same way you just learned what you did learn.

And you won't forget it, like you forgot 99% of the stuff in the syllabus.

So here's the third element of the New Theory: work backward. Start with the problem and go wherever it takes you.

That's the theory that's been evolving for me over all my years of teaching. Don't let an "expert" stand in front of people and tell them everything s/he knows. This is mostly just an ego trip for the expert, and a very boring experience for the victims. The overhead projector has done more to destroy learning than any other thing I can think of.

Part IV:
The Epilogue

I realize that there's an awful lot about education in this little book. But I have only two real passions (that I can discuss openly) in life. These are passions that I would be proud to see mentioned on my tombstone. I'd like it to say: "Rest in Peace. He was a wacko, but he did manage to reduce the number of automobile accidents—and he helped revolutionize the stupid way that education was being done."

So, here are my last thoughts on education—some of which came out of a conversation I had with the carpenter who was rebuilding my back porch, Ricky C. (Rick is a most unusual guy. One of the "unusualities" is that his kids are home-schooled, mostly due to his very unpleasant experience in the wrongheaded school systems that we currently seem to believe in.)

1. Rick was continually intimidated by school because he wasn't one of the few kids who was able and/or willing to remember and regurgitate. (He is instead a brilliant musician, an excellent carpenter, and a person of great integrity; I'd rather have a planet of Ricks than a planet of left brained lawyers.) Why do we intimidate kids? If you've had any experience with kids, you know that their egos are very fragile. Why intimidate them? Why spend so much time showing them what they don't know instead of encouraging them for what they do know? School should not be a place of intimidation. It should be, and can be, fun. In my humble opinion, schools have evolved to what they now are simply because of the ego stroking that the context provides for the teachers. They don't care who learns anything. They want to show how smart they are.

2. Kids already have a reality of their own. And it's a hell of a lot more interesting than learning the capitals of all the Latin American countries. MOTIVATION IS EVERYTHING! Most of us can learn just about anything if and when we decide we want to know about it.

Why do we insist on fabricating an artificial reality for people? Schools should be places where there are people who are willing to guide kids through learning what they— the kids—decide they'd like to know.

Education should be exploration. A chance for people (of all ages) to explore whatever they want to explore. Who are you to tell me what I want to explore? If you want to help me explore something of my choosing, fine. Otherwise, get the hell out of the way, and take your silly teachers' manuals with you. And one more thing: don't let the doorknob hit you in the ass on the way out.

3. As part of the exploration, let's admit that it does not require a three-month college course in chemistry (and a multimillion-dollar chem lab) for me to decide whether I want to know about chemistry.

Rather, how about a 3-WEEK "course" which involves what chemistry is all about, who uses chemistry, what do they use it FOR, what kinds of jobs do they have, what's it like to spend every day doing what they do? Let me spend a few days with people who are doing chemistry; tell me what they and others like them have accomplished.

In 3 weeks, I'll know what I need to know. Save the multimillion-dollar lab for the people who decide that they love it! Classes will now be much smaller and more personalized. (Of course, the "system" won't like this. Now, instead of 15 chemistry professors, they'll only need 4. Enrollments and tuitions will go way down—because only the truly interested will be there. The socializers will be somewhere else.)

This is what "college" should be: an exploration. How can we possibly ask an 18-year-old kid to pick a major? "OK, 18-year-old, snot-nosed kid who doesn't know diddly squat about the world, what do you want to do with the rest of your life?" The kid—trained as he has been to follow the rules—picks something he knows nothing about. Instead of saying, "How the hell should I know?" (And, under his breath, "You jerk!")

OK, I'm almost finished. I hope all this strikes a chord. I hope you realize that education is all wrong and that "they" aren't going to fix it. We (that's WE; i.e., you and me) will need to develop new organizations to do the exploration part of "college." Organizations that will help the snot-nosed kids (and not-so-snot-nosed adults who are in the wrong jobs) to find out how they want to spend their lives—and, in the case of the kids, give them a more reasonably priced place to socialize.

OK, I'm done. Thanks for listening. Call or write if you're interested.

The Value of a Good Education: (Dwayne and the Five Engineers)

(Tom)

Just a short story that will allow all you practical (as opposed to theoretical) types to snicker, chortle, and jeer.

It is many years ago in a galaxy far, far away (actually Cambridge, Mass., about 1972). My brother—then in his second or third senior year at MIT—has just gotten married, and he and his bride (the lovely Marilyn Garelnick) have rented what they think is an apartment. (Their pal from VISTA, Bill Rota, referred to it as a Dumpster with windows.)

It needs painting. It actually needs everything (probably a fire would do it the most good; but painting is cheap and requires little, if any, skill). So Raymond enlists all his pals and his brother to paint. Saturday is the big day. By the time we get organized (buy the paint, brushes, rollers, pans, etc., and have coffee—or, as it was referred to in those days, "have a smoke, a Coke, and a joke"—we get a late start.

But we paint. It gets late, we continue to paint.

It's getting dark. We paint.

It gets darker.

Finally, someone decides to turn on the light. It doesn't work. We see why. The bare bulb is hanging from the ceiling by one wire. The other wire is disconnected.

Now, you should know that the pals and the brother who are helping Raymond are all MIT graduates or almost graduates. These are guys who scored 800s on their SAT exams. These were geniuses, by most measures. Geniuses who had been trained at the most prestigious institute of technological expertise on Mass Avenue in Cambridge. An institute of higher learning attracting brilliant students from the world over.

So the wire is disconnected. So connect it, you might say. Sure, but who's going to do it? "Won't you get zapped if you touch the 'hot' wire?" someone says.

"No, you won't get zapped. Not if you only touch one wire, because you won't be grounded," says another.

"But if you stand on that metal chair, won't that be a ground? Then you'll get zapped, won't you?" says another.

Did I mention that of the 5 "brilliant" people, 3 of them had degrees from MIT in ELECTRICAL ENGINEERING!

We stand there. We ponder. We disagree. We argue. It's getting darker.

Then in comes Dwayne, who lives upstairs. Now, Dwayne is an interesting individual. Dwayne, too, is a graduate—of the eighth grade. Dwayne is in construction; he shovels dirt for a living. Dwayne has very few teeth.

Dwayne walks in and says, "Eh, what are youse guys

doin' in the dark?" At which point he looks up, sees the problem, jumps onto the metal chair, and connects the disconnected wire. All is light.

This would have been funny if it weren't so sad. And so expensive.

This page intentionally left blank.

don't you wish you knew why?

This page intentionally left blank.

don't you wish there

had been more of them?

DATE DUE

JUL 0 6 2000	JAN 1 3
OCT 1 8	
8 / 12	

GAYLORD   PRINTED IN U.S.A.